the most important thing

Also by Adyashanti

Emptiness Dancing

The End of Your World:
Uncensored Straight Talk on the Nature of Enlightenment

Falling into Grace: Insights on the End of Suffering

My Secret Is Silence: Poetry and Sayings of Adyashanti

Resurrecting Jesus: Embodying the Spirit of a Revolutionary Mystic

True Meditation: Discover the Freedom of Pure Awareness

The Way of Liberation: A Practical Guide to Spiritual Enlightenment

ADYASHANTI

the most imp●rtant thing

DISCOVERING TRUTH AT THE HEART OF LIFE

sounds true
BOULDER, COLORADO

Sounds True
Boulder, CO 80306

© 2019 Adyashanti

SOUNDS TRUE is a trademark of Sounds True, Inc.
Published 2019

Cover design by Jennifer Miles
Book design by Beth Skelley

Printed in Canada

Library of Congress Cataloging-in-Publication Data
Names: Adyashanti, author.
Title: The most important thing : discovering truth at the heart of life /
  Adyashanti.
Description: Boulder, CO : Sounds True, [2019]
Identifiers: LCCN 2018016712 (print) | LCCN 2018035036 (ebook) |
  ISBN 9781683641926 (ebook) | ISBN 9781683641919 (hardcover)
Subjects: LCSH: Self-realization. | Meditation. | Self.
Classification: LCC BF637.S4 (ebook) | LCC BF637.S4 A369 2019 (print) |
  DDC 158.1—dc23
LC record available at https://lccn.loc.gov/2018016712

10 9 8 7 6 5 4 3 2 1

Contents

ACKNOWLEDGMENTS . . . vii

INTRODUCTION . . . 1

WHAT IS THE MOST IMPORTANT THING? . . . 4

THE POWER OF A GOOD QUESTION . . . 9

WHAT ARE YOU IN SERVICE TO? . . . 14

THE DOORWAY OF DIFFICULTY . . . 20

THE INTERSECTION OF LOVE AND GRACE . . . 26

WILLINGNESS TO TRUST THE UNKNOWN . . . 30

AN ELEMENT OF SURPRISE . . . 34

THE FUNDAMENTAL REALIZATION . . . 38

CHALLENGED BY THE GREAT SORROW OF THE WORLD . . . 43

VITAL MOMENTS . . . 49

DEEP WISDOM IN UNCERTAINTY . . . 52

LIFE IS A SERIES OF UNKNOWN MOMENTS . . . 57

MEETING THE BUDDHA ON THE ROAD . . . 63

THE DIRTY LITTLE SECRET OF SPIRITUAL PRACTICE . . . 71

WILLINGNESS TO ENCOUNTER SILENCE . . . 75

THE HEART OF CONTEMPLATION . . . 81

ALWAYS ALREADY MEDITATING . . . 87

WHEN THE UNIVERSE CONTEMPLATES ITSELF . . . 92

CONSCIOUS OF CONSCIOUSNESS . . . 98

KNOW THYSELF . . . 107

YOU ARE THE TOTAL ENVIRONMENT . . . 112

EXPERIENCE PRIOR TO THOUGHT . . . 115

THE SIMPLE JOY OF BEING . . . 120

PRISTINE BUDDHA MIND . . . 127

BEING STILL . . . 134

EXPLORING BIRTH, LIFE, AND DEATH . . . 139

YOU ARE THE BUDDHA . . . 149

ABOUT THE AUTHOR . . . 157

Acknowledgments

A few years back I was sitting around the dinner table at my home with Tami Simon, founder of Sounds True, and Mitchell Clute, an editor and producer who has been intimately involved with every Sounds True project I have done in recent years. I shared with them my fantasy of someday having a little recording studio at my home, so I could pop in and record teachings whenever the spirit hit me. To my great surprise, Tami said, "Let's make that happen, Adya. Where would you put it?" After I recovered from my shock, I thought about it for a moment and said there was a little closet space under the stairway that might work. Tami then asked, "So what do you want to do next with Sounds True?"

After some time brainstorming, we came up with the idea to record a series of talks about how grace arises in the ordinary moments of everyday life. The program was titled *Moments of Grace*, and from the very start this project felt to be perfumed with grace. I cannot thank Tami enough for her friendship and generosity, as well as for her constant invitation and encouragement to produce whatever teachings I feel inspired to with Sounds True. You are a great grace in my life as well as a true dharma friend. And a great bow of appreciation as well to Mitchell Clute, who has faithfully guided not only this book but all of my Sounds True projects to fruition. Your dedication and wisdom inform everything I do with Sounds True, and I appreciate you from the bottom of my heart.

I want to extend a mountain of gratitude to Alice Peck, who had the Herculean task of editing and arranging my spontaneous ramblings into a comprehensible manuscript. Your task was great, and you performed it with tremendous care and dedication. My appreciation for you runs deep and wide.

I also want to offer a deep bow of thanks to Jennifer Miles for her wonderful cover design. I cannot comprehend how, out of nowhere, you pull from your creative spirit such fine artwork over and over again. May your wellspring of creativity continue to flow forevermore.

And, finally, I want to express my heartfelt appreciation to Aron Arnold, studio manager at Sounds True, for turning my little closet space under the stairwell into a wonderful recording studio. May many years of recordings flow forth as a result of your making my little fantasy into a reality.

Adyashanti
Los Gatos, California
2018

Introduction

OUR INNER LIVES ARE EVERY BIT AS ASTONISHING,
BAFFLING, AND MYSTERIOUS AS THE INFINITE
VASTNESS OF THE COSMOS.

As long as cognitively capable human beings have been living on this small blue planet among the stars, they have been telling stories. Storytelling began long ago with our ancestors sitting around the safety of an open fire on moonlit nights recalling the events of the day, or of the year, or of their distant relatives. And even though we have developed technology beyond anything our ancestors might have imagined, we still tell stories to one another every day and, in our own minds, perhaps nearly every minute. Each moment of our lives is a story in creation, a novel without end, where new chapters are being lived out daily. And if we are paying attention, we'll notice that some of those stories contain moments of grace when we are gifted with wisdom or love and understanding. Such stories can enlighten and transform our lives for the better.

In 2017, I began recording a weekly series for Sounds True called *Moments of Grace*, through which I hoped to convey some of those wisdom stories from my own life. As I recorded stories that had gifted me with a bit of insight or a better understanding of love, I began to notice a theme emerging. In one way or another, each of the stories I told showed me how vital it was to be oriented toward an awareness of what I call "the most important thing." Time and again, each story that conveyed meaning in my life was an expression of the essential importance of being able to discern what truly mattered in life. Every story seemed to hone my ability to discern the most important thing about each situation I had experienced. In retelling these impactful stories from my life, I was also reliving and reexamining the paradoxical power of intention and grace.

As the weeks went by, I eventually found myself stretching my lifelong bad memory to its limits as I tried to recall stories from my past that had shaped my character and my life. If truth be told, I rarely live in the past, but by recording the *Moments of Grace* series I had the opportunity to experience again some of the significant stories from my life and reconsider their impact. It was a wonderful and clarifying experience, and as the project went on, I began to turn more toward elucidating the wisdom and love that I had gained through these stories and how one could find that same wellspring of wisdom and love within oneself.

For each of our lives provides all that we need to gain deeper wisdom and love—if only we can learn to not become captivated by the negative and confusing spin that the mind often creates, but instead derive useful and enlightening knowledge from our own direct experience. This requires a disciplined awareness of and keen attention to the moment-to-moment experience of being, as well as great honesty and sincerity of heart. I've found that only by taking complete responsibility for my moment-to-moment experience of being do I retain both a sense of sovereignty and a feeling of connectedness with whomever I may be in relationship to. It seems that the experience of grace, when new vistas of insight and understanding spontaneously open within us, is intimately related to (though not directly caused by) the intentions and priorities that we live by. This paradox of intention and grace is embodied within the unfolding of each of our lives as well as in the stories and teachings of this book.

Our inner lives are every bit as astonishing, baffling, and mysterious as the infinite vastness of the cosmos. For we are each individual expressions of conscious being, and we contain the vastness of the cosmos within us, as much as we are contained within it. To look within and answer the ancient call to *know thyself* is perhaps the greatest and strangest adventure of all. It is the key to awakening to the truth of our being and living the most evolved lives that we can individually and collectively imagine. My hope is that this book will not only entertain and uplift you but will also give you the tools to dive deeply into the immediate experience of being, so that you will find your own experience of grace by attending to the most important thing.

What Is the
Most Important Thing?

NO SPIRITUAL TEACHER, NO MATTER HOW WISE, AND
NO TEACHING, NO MATTER HOW PROFOUND, CAN BE A
SUBSTITUTE FOR DISCOVERING WHAT IS IMPORTANT TO YOU.

What is the most important thing to you? Not the top ten, not the top five, not the top three, not the top two, but *the* top. Is it awakening? Is it love? Is it peace? I could go on naming possibilities, but think about your spiritual life, the part of you that deep dives into the discovery of meaning. By "meaning," I am not referring to the meaning of life—that ends up being theoretical. I am talking about meaning as that which gives us a sense of vitality, aliveness, inspiration, calm, and joy.

I have done some research on the idea of the most important thing, and I have looked at it from different angles, talking to executives, athletes, musicians, writers, artists of all kinds, and anybody who excels at something. For as long as I can remember, I have been interested in people who do things well. These people tend to have an ability to define what is most important, to know it within their being, and to rally their resources toward it. If you think about it, anybody who achieves unusual excellence—you could throw Warren Buffett, Miles Davis, Michelangelo, or the Buddha and Jesus and other spiritual figures in there—has a sense of direction and a genuine feeling for the most important thing in their life.

The Buddha's most important thing was his recognition of the human condition, which involves suffering: sickness, old age, and death. He asked, "Is there any resolution to this immense issue of suffering for any human being?" He oriented his whole life around this question. He left his wife, his children, and his position in society. He walked away from it all and became a sadhu, a renunciant. Most of us are not going to do that. That is fine, because to copy what somebody else did is one of the mistakes we make. We should not say, "If the Buddha left everything behind, I need to leave everything behind." What is more important than the renunciation is the Buddha's focus, the sense that he found *his most important thing*. His act of leaving everything to pursue his question is unimportant; it is his response to the question that matters. For Jesus, I would say it was to put God first in all things—that was his most important thing.

There is a clarity that comes from finding out what the most important thing is to you. When I talk to people, especially when I am teaching, I often ask, "So what is your spiritual life all about? What is the focus? What do you want?" People answer, "Enlightenment," to which I reply, "What does that mean to you? What is the enlightenment that you seek?" I explain, "I am not talking about the 'sales pitch' for enlightenment. I am not talking about what someone promised enlightenment would give you." The sales pitch may promise eternal bliss, an end to unhappiness or suffering, and a life that is kind and benevolent, in which everybody loves and appreciates you. That has little to do with what enlightenment is.

I am asking people to tell me, not what they have been sold, but what they want. When they think about the most important thing they are seeking, what does that mean? Spirituality is my discipline, but you can apply this question to any area of life—to relationships, art, sports, or play. We are rarely taught to do this. Instead, our culture, family, and friends tell us what the most important things in life are, and we accept and absorb these stories without a lot of reflection.

If we never question, then we focus our life on whatever we are conditioned to focus on, until one day we realize: *What I have focused on was not that important to me.* A reorienting follows when people hit midlife, because it is a time when we have done enough, achieved enough, or run the rat race long enough to start to wonder if it is satisfactory. *Is it enough?* That is when we reexamine and begin to ask questions: *Is that what I want? What is the most important thing for me?*

When I ask people, "What is your spiritual life all about?" you would be surprised by how few have taken the time or imposed the mental discipline to define it. They read book after book, work with teacher after teacher, and even do years of meditation or other spiritual practice, yet they are chasing something that somebody else defined for them, thinking, *That sounds pretty good. I'll go for that.* But they are not discovering the unique orientation that belongs only to them and their life. Nobody can give this to them. No spiritual teacher, no matter how wise, and no teaching, no matter how profound, can be a substitute for discovering what is important to you.

When I ask people about their most important thing, their eyes go up, left, and right as if they are searching their memory for an answer to this question, but if we know our most important thing, our reply is immediate. We do not have to think about it—it is there. Such people know what they are doing and why they are doing it. They know the most important thing.

When I look back and reflect upon this idea of the thing that orients my life, my source of inspiration and aspiration, I see that it was an unfolding of what was important to me *at that time.* We all have phases in life during which different things are important. There are aspects of us that sustain their importance throughout a whole lifetime, and there are things that play themselves out, leading us to move on to the next thing. You could apply this concept to any moment and ask, *What is the most important thing right now?* Not the thing that comes from your head or even from your heart, but from deep down in your gut. *What is it?*

I looked back at everything at which I ever excelled. When I was young I was dyslexic, and in first grade I had a hard time reading. I made a decision. I discovered my most important thing at that time: I was going to learn to read as well as everybody else. My parents engaged a tutor for me, and I worked, and I worked, and I had a focus. In less than a year, I was up to speed in reading. By the time I was in high school, I was reading at college level. This was because I had found the most important thing to me, knew it was important, and backed it up with action. Action is the second part of this process—doing something about the most important thing, not just thinking about and hoping for it.

Later in life I got into various forms of athletics. When I was eighteen, I raced bikes at a fairly high level, and for a time that became the most important thing. It inspired me; it drew upon my deepest resources. I focused on racing and was willing to do whatever it took to excel. I did not have problems with motivation; I did not have problems with wanting to train. At that time, I was riding my bicycle between 300 and 400 miles a week. Even when the weather was windy and stormy, I rode my bike in the pouring rain, sometimes for four or five hours at a stretch. To motivate myself I would think about how 80 or 90 percent of my competitors were not riding. Though they might work out on their indoor trainer for an hour or so, most of them would not ride outside in a storm. *But I did.* I used that as a motivation. I concentrated my desire on my most important thing, rode my bike in horrendous conditions, and because of that focus I excelled.

Everything that I excelled in throughout my life came about because it was my most important thing. I knew why I was there, what I was doing, what I was inspired by, and what I was looking for; I knew what the most important thing was. When it came to spirituality, I realized there are many different ideas about what a spiritual life should be. I found I had to disconnect from how others defined it and keep returning to what truly belonged to me. I avoided the sales pitch for enlightenment, as I was not looking to achieve a lot of the things we imagine spirituality is about. I wanted to know what truth was—the deepest, most fundamental truth of existence—and to make a positive contribution to life. *What is this thing called truth, called enlightenment?* This was my question and my driving obsession. This desire for truth has been with me in different ways for as long as I can remember.

What about you? What is the most important thing in your life? Do not assume it is the first idea that pops into your mind. Discovering it may take some real investigation and some serious contemplation. It will be worth the effort and can be a turning point in whatever area of your life you apply it. When you dig down, when you impose a mental discipline and do not settle for the quick, easy answer that you may well have learned from somebody else, you will find what nobody can give you and what belongs to you alone. I am not asking you to tell me what you believe *I think* should be your most important thing, because that is not for me to define for anybody. That is for each person to define for themselves. You need to impose discipline—and when I say "discipline," I mean you may have to think this through and meditate on it for days or months to get a true sense of what it is.

As a spiritual teacher, I have seen that to define the most important thing *is* the most important thing. It is the first step. Until you do, your life does not even belong to you.

The Power of a
Good Question

Here's a wonderful quote that I came upon by the nineteenth-century French writer Pierre-Marc-Gaston de Lévis: "It is easier to judge the mind of a man by his questions rather than his answers." I love this kind of thinking because it turns our way of looking at things upside down. We are oriented to what I call "consensus reality"—what most people agree upon—but finding the most important thing depends on not accepting the ideas, beliefs, and opinions of others, because the way most people go about life does not always lead to great depth, joy, inspiration, or peace.

The questions that we ask are so incredibly important. *What is the most important thing in my spiritual life? What is my entire spiritual life oriented around?* You could apply this line of questioning to your relationships. *What is my friendship or romance all about? What is the most important thing about that person to me?* Or the subject of your investigation could be work. *What is the most important thing about my livelihood?* Because we are accessing our depth with these kinds of questions, it is not always an easy or comfortable process. You must be willing to go against the grain, against consensus reality, and against what everybody thinks is the true and correct answer.

As Lévis suggested, the answers are not as important as the questions—but our conditioning is around answers. When we are in school and it comes time to take a test, we want to get the right answer; we want to regurgitate what we were taught. That is what is expected, and it is part of learning. Unfortunately, at least to my thinking, it is too big a part of education, because we are taught to fill ourselves with other people's answers and not to find our own. Some of this is the result of practical necessity—memorizing certain answers helps us to learn how to read, do math, and understand the sciences. But when it comes to our lives, to our sense of happiness and well-being and love, when it comes to what we contribute to this precious and brief life, repeating other people's answers doesn't help us answer the big questions: What do you want to contribute? What *are* you contributing? What is important to *you*?

I am a big lover of asking profound and deep questions. I call this "inquiry." Questioning is not safe; answers are safe. Accepting someone else's answers is safe, an ideology is safe, and a theology is safe. We seek the "right" answers because we think they will make us comfortable, protect us, and insulate us from suffering. We grasp at the first thing that makes us feel better, but truth may or may not make you feel better—some truths are beautiful, and some are shocking. However, a great vitality comes with discovering any truth, because that which is real is charged with life-force, energy, and power.

Usually, when we want to get to know someone, we are looking for answers. "What is your job? What do you do for pleasure? What movies do you like? What is your favorite book?" We want to know, and that is fine, as that is part of human communication. But asking somebody what their most important question in life is can be a much better way of getting to know them than asking about their occupation or where they live.

It is our questions that have power if we want to live an inspired life and a life that feels like it has great meaning to us. I am not talking about the conventional sense of "meaning," like when we say, "This is the meaning of my life" and then we define that, nor am I talking about something practical, like "Four is the sum of two plus two." I am talking instead about the living feeling of meaning—the experience of being extraordinarily alive, here, and present. That is a profound meaning, even if it is a meaning you cannot put into words, because it is an experience and not a definition.

Questions bring us closer to that experience, though they are often paradoxical: when we first ask them, the immediate answer is a conditioned response. To dig deeply into these questions, to look deep inside oneself, is its own spiritual practice. *What is the most important thing?* So many of the answers that we have within us are there because at some point they made us feel comfortable or safe or secure, but they did so at the expense of a rich experience of being, existing, living, and even doing. The cost of not asking insightful questions is that we tend to live on automatic pilot and solely from our conditioning, most of which was imprinted in us by our culture and society, our family and friends, the education we have had, and the consensus reality that most everybody falls into without even knowing it. Anybody who is involved in any kind of excellence or profound achievement tends to question consensus reality, especially spiritual people like the Buddha or Jesus or so many others. They do not settle for a comforting belief system, and they do not comply because the authorities have suggested that is the way the world works or that is what is true; they explore these issues within themselves.

The great mythologist Joseph Campbell paraphrased Carl Jung, saying that religion is here to protect us from the truly religious experience. How does it do that? By telling us the way everything is within an ideology of theology or a belief system. We respond, "Okay, that sounds good to me, I'll buy into it, that is the way things are," but doing that disconnects us from true revelation, because the place where revelation occurs within us is in the unknown. Dogma fills the unknown within us with the known; religion fills us all up, and we walk around with a new ideology, which precludes having meaningful religious or spiritual experiences. This does not mean that religious people do not have religious or spiritual experiences. They do, but they have them *despite* their beliefs, not because of them. Although they may have a belief system, they continue to reach beyond dogma and beyond mere ideas.

It does not matter what the belief is—theistic, nontheistic, dualistic, nondualistic. It is our answers that blind us, that we hide behind, and that we use to protect ourselves from the great insecurity of facing our confusion and our doubt and plunging into our consciousness in a profound way.

Even if we know not to accept the answers we are given, the questions we ask can also be conditioned. Sometimes the questions that are useful are the ones that are dangerous—the ones that feel like they threaten your consensus reality. The right kinds of questions will shake up your world view. When you ask those kinds of questions, you will begin to find that the ways you have defined yourself limited you and that they are not who and what you are. This kind of questioning is big questioning.

Deep spirituality orbits around the existential questions, and we each have our own. Yours may be: *What is my place in the universe? What is God? What is life? What in the hell is going on here?* For me it was a common spiritual question—*Who am I?*—that challenged my assumptions. One day, early in my spiritual practice, the question appeared during meditation. I thought, *Wait a minute. I do not even know who I am. I do not even know who the "I" is that is seeking enlightenment. If I do not know who I am, on what basis am I asking any other question?* It occurred to me I was chasing enlightenment, but I did not even know *who* was chasing enlightenment. I realized I had better get straight on who I was. Suddenly everything was put into a different context—the enlightenment I was looking for did not seem as important as who was looking for it. That question was unsettling when it came to me. Like a slap in the face, it rearranged my priority system, because it was a deeper question than the ones I had been asking myself. As soon as this came to me, I knew I had found my orientation; I had found my most important thing in my spiritual life.

When we find that most important thing, it comes to us with a great intensity that makes us feel insecure, because it calls *everything* into question. It is disquieting, but at the same time it is inspirational, because when we ask a question of true importance, there is great energy and an expansive quality to it. Usually the true answers to these existential questions are not ones you can write down in a book; they are more like revelations than answers. It is like the way you cannot truly describe the experience of drinking a glass of water to somebody who has never had a glass of water; the best thing you can do is hand them a glass of water so they can experience it for themselves. *Water!* Telling them what it is like is not going to be the same.

This is what important questions do. They open a space within us, clearing away the preconceived debris so that something new and transformative can arise. That is what I want to offer you: your questions—the beauty of them, the inspiration of them, the insecurity of them—because that is where your potential and your revelation lie. In fact, as a spiritual teacher, I have discovered that one of the most important things I can do is question the assumption people have that deep spiritual awakening is an uncommon event. Even ardent students believe it is extraordinary and difficult. But what if it is not all that rare and difficult? What if those beliefs are not true? Question your assumptions, lean far into the unknown. Question it all. When we do, we realize the awakening we seek is possible.

What Are You in Service To?

IT IS NOT ABOUT BEING A NICE PERSON;
IT IS SOMETHING FAR DEEPER THAN THAT.

What am I in service to? This is one of my favorite questions. It is an awakener. It is an awareness practice and an honesty practice. It is one of the big questions, up there with *What am I giving myself to? What is my life about? Who am I?* and *What is God?* If we are not asking these bigger questions, we tend to sleepwalk through life, skimming the surface, and acting and reacting from entrenched points of view and patterns of behaving.

Service is not a strictly spiritual idea or ideal; part of the human experience is to serve and to give back. To be human is to help in some way and to nurture the well-being of others. One of the beautiful things about service is that we are simultaneously taking part in the well-being of ourselves. This points to something essential about service: when it is done from a sense of wholeness, when it comes from an overflow and a sharing of an inner abundance, it is enriching and life affirming—not only for us, but for anybody involved in whatever we are trying to serve.

When I think about service, I think about my first teacher, Arvis Joen Justi. In my twenties, I became interested in Zen Buddhism through a book I read by Alan Watts. I cannot remember which one it was, but at the time, in the early 1980s, Watts was a popular writer and one of the first people to bring Eastern spiritual teachings to the West. His book led me to one by Ram Dass, *Journey of Awakening*. In the back of that book was a directory of spiritual and contemplative centers throughout the United States. At that time, there were few Zen monasteries, or temples, or yoga retreats, so the list fit on a couple of pages; nowadays it would take volumes. One of the centers was the Los Gatos Zen Group, which was about fifteen minutes from where I lived in Northern California. I was over the moon! I had no idea what this group was or anything about it, but I telephoned and talked to the woman who became my teacher—Arvis.

She gave me directions to her place in the foothills in Los Gatos. Even though it was near my home, the location seemed obscure, and I got lost a few times on the way. When I finally arrived, it was a house. I do not know what I was expecting, but I do not think I was expecting a regular house! I was not sure if I had the right address, so I checked and rechecked. Finally, I got out of my car and walked up the driveway. A small note hung on the door. It said, "Zazen" and had an arrow pointing toward the back of the building. I knew "zazen" was the Zen term for meditation, so I figured I must be in the right place.

I walked around to the backyard, climbed the stairs, and arrived at some sliding glass doors at the rear of the house. The whole thing was unusual. A woman in her late fifties or early sixties opened the back door, and I saw another sign. This one said: "Please remove your shoes." I kicked my shoes off and looked up at the woman to find out what to do next. All she did was stare down at my shoes. I stared too and then realized how haphazardly I had kicked them off—one on top of the other. They were not placed with attention, or mindfulness, or care. I received her silent message. I reached down and arranged my shoes neatly next to each other. She smiled a big smile and said, "Welcome!"

I received a full teaching from Arvis in those first awkward moments. When she drew my attention to how carelessly I had treated my shoes, she gave me my first lesson in what it means to be aware, to be present to everything instead of to a few chosen things that you consider important. It is all about paying attention, about being extraordinarily conscious of what is happening inside you and all around you. It was a wonderful, complete teaching that still speaks to me decades later.

I meditated with Arvis that day, and I kept coming back. Over time I saw the great amount of devotion and service she offered. She opened her house to strangers for more than thirty years. Her living room was set up for meditation—black cushions laid out on top of black mats and a small bodhisattva figure at the front of the room. Everything was understated and simple. Arvis cleared her schedule every Sunday and prepared a talk. She did not ask for anything in return. I was impressed by her quiet, humble way and the tremendous strength beneath her humility—a reservoir of clarity and wisdom, of a more awakened way of seeing and experiencing.

I will never stop reflecting upon the great devotion Arvis had to serving something that was important—something she loved. When she first started to offer teachings at her house, she would sit down after preparing everything, but nobody would show up. Still, she wrote a talk, set up her meditation room, and opened her house every single week, week after week. Sometimes, out of compassion, her husband would sit with her, but mostly she sat alone.

She continued to do this for an entire year without a single person coming. That is dedication! What service to the dharma, the Buddhist teachings—not being in service to how many people appear, to numbers or normal measures of success, but to doing what she was called to do. After a year, one person came, and for the next year it was Arvis and that one person. They sat together each Sunday morning, and Arvis gave her talk to an audience of one. As word slowly spread, more people arrived, until sometimes she would have fifteen or twenty people.

Her dedication was a great teaching for me. It touched my heart because it spoke to what service is: the willingness to put ourselves in a position of giving, to be an embodiment of what we are dedicated to, and to put our life, time, attention, and energy into the most important things. Even when Arvis was sitting in her living room alone, she was in service to all the people who might show up in the future.

Many years later, I ended up being one of those people.

Arvis was willing to serve the dharma quietly and humbly. She did not need the temple, robes, and official ceremonies, although when it came to the Buddhist teachings she could be extremely direct; there was no messing around, and you could see her dedication to the truth. Arvis spent more than thirty years carrying on a lineage of truth teaching, as her teacher, Taizan Maezumi Roshi, and his teacher, Hakuun Yasutani, and his teacher's teachers had done for more than a thousand years. These were people who served what they loved. From her point of view, even when sitting alone she had great company—a long lineage of dharma teachers.

In the present moment, we are all serving in our own way; we are all being part of a lineage. Whether we want to or not, we are all passing something on, and we are all affecting one another, consciously or unconsciously. But do not just ask yourself what lineage you came from; inquire into your lineage going forward. What are you contributing to? What are you serving?

It is so easy for us in the West. We are so conditioned to be in the consumer mind-set, always asking, *What can this do for me?*—as in, *What can this movie do for me? What can this person do for me?* If it is a spiritual teaching: *What can this teaching do for me?* If it is a walk in the woods: *What can this walk do for me?* It is an attitude, and it is a stance. What gets lost is the acknowledgment that we are taking part in one another's lives; we are affecting the world and the beings around us. This brings up the whole notion of what we are in service *to*. What is our life an expression of? What is our contribution?

Even though it is not especially hip or popular nowadays, this idea of the necessity of service has been a part of every spiritual or religious tradition. It is not about being a nice person; it is something far deeper than that. It is about connecting to what is important in our lives—to what has been called "the deathbed virtues." David Brooks, a commentator and author, distinguishes between "résumé virtues" and "eulogy virtues." Résumé virtues are the things you tell someone like an employer when you are trying to sell yourself. They are what you have accomplished and succeeded at, what you are good at, and what makes you money. Then, as Brooks said, there are our eulogy virtues—the ones you might want mentioned when you are being remembered at your funeral. Our eulogy virtues connect us to the deepest part of ourselves: the effect we have on people and life around us.

Contemplating eulogy virtues helps us look inward and circles us back to the notion of service. *What am I in service to? How can I be in service to the deepest thing I know?* Contemplate this. Sit with the questions and be with them in quietness. Our most important thing may be truth, freedom, enlightenment, love, or compassion. We find what is important when we look at what we devote our time and attention to. Time and attention are our two most precious and guarded commodities as modern human beings. Think about it: most of us will give our money to a cause before we give our time and attention to it.

I am not suggesting that we impose a new idea of what we "should" be doing: "I should be contributing in this way. I should be contributing in that way." The "should" obscures the natural goodness and inspiring energy of the heart, and so we must be on the lookout for our mind turning service into obligation. It is more about every moment of clarity, insight, or revelation having as its corollary a possibility to be put into action or to be in some way expressed. We think in big terms—it seems like today everybody wants to change the world—and sometimes I get the feeling that a lot of people do not want to be bothered with taking part in service to something unless they can create a public, visible effect or unless their actions can have a cosmic significance. That is not service; it is egotistical self-aggrandizement. Real service is a humble energy. It is looking for where you can serve the thing you love. *How can I participate in what I love? How can I be a living expression of what I love?* Not in a perfect way—you can disappear into a lot of self-judgment if you look at it through that lens—but in aspirational, small ways.

There is another way of looking at service. When Arvis silently directed my attention to how I had placed my shoes, she gave me a glimpse of how being in service to one thing is reflective of how I am in service to everything else. She demonstrated the importance of not dividing the world into "These things are worthy of my attention and my love and my service, but these other things are not," which is looking through a dualistic and self-centered lens.

People sometimes say to me, "Well, you are a spiritual teacher, so you get to serve all the time." Imagine if the only time I was in service—the only time I served the dharma—was when I was onstage in front of a bunch of people. That would be extremely limited. It would make me a performer, and my dharma would be an act—something I did not do in the rest of my life. I teach because my teacher asked me to, because I was called to do it, and so I do it joyfully even when it is challenging, or I am tired, or I am getting on another plane and I have to be away from home. There is a reason behind all of this: I am serving something I see as truly valuable.

However, that is not the only avenue of service, for me or for others. Much is in the moment-to-moment unfolding of human life: the encounters with the world around us, with the way we place our shoes, with the next person we talk with, with the next situation we are in. During those moments in your own life, ask: *What am I in service to?* When we are serving the qualities of life that we consider most valuable, there is a fringe benefit, as we tend to be far happier when we are in service to the things we love than when we are just trying to acquire more of what we love.

If you are in the position of a consumer, you feel "less than": there is a feeling of not enough, of *I need more and I want more*, and it leaves you feeling inadequate. Instead, start your day thinking, *Today I am going to undertake one act of service for somebody or something as an expression of what I value in my heart and of what I love. I am going to make a gesture in that direction, even if it is only a small one.* You will be amazed how wonderful it feels to take part in and be aligned with service. We are never in as much joy as when we are engaged in the well-being of others. That is one of the beautiful things about serving, along with the possibility that someone or something else may benefit. I find myself in a real state of gratitude and appreciation for anybody who has been in service to me or to something important, like Arvis was to the dharma for all those years. That gratitude allows me to do what I do. It fills me with a wonderful feeling and inspiration when I ask, *What am I in service to?*

The Doorway of Difficulty

UNMASKING *IS* THE SPIRITUAL PATH.

After meditating with Arvis for some time, I decided to do a week-long silent Zen meditation retreat. Arvis said, "I feel good about a teacher named Jakusho Kwong up at Sonoma Mountain Zen Center. Maybe that would be a good place for you to go." I was excited to experience an authentic retreat in a Zen Buddhist temple with all the accoutrements—the bells, the robes, the rituals, the whole thing.

I got there in the late afternoon, and the retreat was scheduled to start in the early evening. After we had dinner, we went into the Zendo for the first meditation session. It was a very formal place, and I had no idea what the etiquette was. There was minimal instruction, so I learned what I was supposed to be doing by watching other people, which heightened my awareness right away. I sat down on my cushion with all my gleeful anticipation about this experience as the temple bell was struck three times to begin the period of meditation.

As soon as that bell rang, adrenaline flooded my body. It was not fear, but my whole system went into fight-or-flight mode. All I could think was, *How do I get out of here? Let me out of here!* which is silly because five seconds earlier I was thrilled about being there.

Fortunately, a small, quiet voice inside me said, *You have no idea how important this is. You must stay.* So even though I had adrenaline rushes twenty-four hours a day for five days and nights in a row, I did not sleep throughout the entire retreat, and I contemplated leaving many times, I managed to hang in there—barely—and finish. Not an auspicious beginning for a future spiritual teacher, but that is what happened. I never knew exactly why I had that reaction, but I have a hunch. When you undertake a retreat like that, something deep within you knows, *Oh, boy, the jig is up now. This is not make-believe. This is the real thing.* Something in me knew that this was going to be a complete life reorientation. I did not realize this consciously, but unconsciously my ego reacted as if threatened: *This is it. This guy is considering the nature of his own being as far as the egoic impulse running the rest of life.*

In some ways, my first retreat was a disaster. The only thing that got me through was a mantra I came up with on the second day. Thousands of times over those five nights and days, I said to myself: *I will never, ever, ever do this again.* That was my big spiritual mantra!

One of the things that impressed me during that retreat was that Kwong—the *roshi*, or teacher—gave a talk each day, and that talk was my respite because I got to sit and listen and be entertained. It was a relief from the bone-jarring meditation, the never-ending silence, and the pain in my knees and back. Kwong had recently returned from a trip to India that had a huge impact on him. I could tell because as he was recounting stories about his trip, tears streamed down his cheeks and dripped off the bottom of his chin.

One story especially touched me. Kwong was walking on a dirt road through an impoverished area. There were some kids playing a game with a ball and a stick out in the middle of the road. One kid stood apart from the group, as if ostracized. This boy was watching the kids play and had a sad look on his face. He had a cleft palate, so his upper lip was severely deformed. Kwong walked up to the boy, but they did not speak the same language, so he did not know what to say. There was a moment of indecision, and then Kwong took the boy's hand in his and with his other hand reached into his pocket and pulled out some money. He pointed to a little shop that sold ice cream and gave the money to the boy. I thought it was a sweet way of giving a little comfort and acknowledging this poor kid's existence, his loneliness.

As Kwong did this, he gestured to the group of children that seemed to have rejected the boy as if to say, "Go get them and buy them ice cream." He had given the child enough money to buy treats for all the kids. The boy waved to them and pointed toward the ice cream shop, and all the children joined this one kid who had been lonely and sad. Suddenly he was the hero! He had money and was buying ice cream for everybody. The kids were laughing and talking with him. He was included in their group.

Kwong sat in full lotus position on his cushion in his beautiful brown teacher's robes and told this story in a resonant, soft voice, deeply touched by the poverty that he saw and by the loneliness of that child. He never hid his tears, and he never seemed embarrassed by his emotion. Watching another man embody this juxtaposition of great strength and tenderness taught me more about true masculinity than anything else in my life. Hearing him speak with such fearlessness was extraordinary. For a young, aspiring Zen student, to have this be my first encounter with a Zen master was a tremendous stroke of good luck and grace, especially since during this whole retreat, except for the talks, I was hanging on by a thread. I continued to study with Kwong, did some retreats with him over the years, and appreciated his great wisdom, but I never again saw him in the state he was in on that first retreat. His openness and dignity were a powerful teaching—it was like being bathed in grace.

Since then I have attended and led hundreds of retreats, but I still look back on that first one with Kwong as both the absolute worst and absolute best in my life. I did not know how powerfully it had affected me until months later. Staying with whatever arose for me despite being flooded with adrenaline, sitting with it in a raw way through all those hours of meditation instead of running away, was profound. When you are having that experience, when you are being pushed to your limit, you do not think of it as grace, but the real grace was that I was in that environment. I was in a place where I could not go anywhere, where I could not turn on the TV or listen to the radio or grab a book or enter a discussion. I had to face the entirety of my experience. Afterward, when I tried to describe the retreat to people, I would end up in tears—not tears of sadness or even of joy, but of depth. I had touched upon something that was so meaningful, vital, and important that it opened my heart.

As we go through life, we eventually have enough experience to see that sometimes profound difficulty can also be profoundly heart opening. When you are in a tough position, when you are facing something hard, when you feel challenged, when you feel like you are at your edge, it is a gift to have the willingness to stop, to sit with those moments, and not to look for the quick, easy resolution for that feeling. It is a kind of grace to be able and willing to open yourself entirely to the experience of challenge, of difficulty, and of insecurity.

There is light grace, and there is dark grace. Light grace is when you have a revelation—when you have insights. Awakening is a light grace; it is like the sun coming out from behind the clouds. The heart opens, and old identities fall away. Then there is dark grace, like what I had on that retreat. I do not mean "dark" in the sense of sinister or evil, but "dark" in the sense of traveling through the darkness looking for light. You cannot see the way through whatever you are experiencing and whatever the challenge is. One of the most amazing things that daily meditation has taught me over many years is to have the wisdom and grace to quietly and silently be with whatever presents itself, whatever is there, without looking for a solution or an explanation.

To see yourself is the heart of what a spiritual discipline like meditation is all about. When people come on retreat with me, we meditate for five or six periods a day. The idea of meditation is not necessarily to get good at it—whatever your definition may be of being "good" at meditation—but the most important thing, the useful thing, the reason we are meditating is so that we encounter ourselves. If you are not using your meditation to hide from your experience or to transcend it or to concentrate your way out of it, if you are being quietly present, meditation forces honesty. It is an extraordinarily truthful way to experience yourself in that moment. This willingness to encounter yourself is vitally important. It is a key to spiritual life and to awakening: being present for whatever is. Sometimes "whatever is" is mundane; sometimes it is full of light, grace, and insight; and sometimes it begins as a dark grace, where we do not know where we are going or how to get through it, and then suddenly there is light.

One of the nice things about meditation is that when we sit with these moments as they arise, we start to trust in them and in the dark grace. We realize that it is in feeling lost that our true nature finds itself. In meditation we encounter ourselves, and it elicits a real honesty *if* we are ready for it. You can read about things forever, you can listen to talks forever, and you can assume that you understand or that you have got it, but if you can be with yourself in a quiet way without running away, that is the necessary honesty. When we can do nothing and be extraordinarily happy and at peace with that, we have found tranquility within ourselves.

Through experience, we find we can trust the moments when we do not know which way to go, when we feel like we will never have the answers. We know we can stop there and listen. This is the heart of meditation: it is the act of listening in a deep way. You could boil all of spirituality down to the art and practice of listening to nothing and trusting in the difficulty. That is what I learned on that first retreat. It taught me that a direct encounter with challenge is a doorway to accessing our depth, coming face-to-face with our most important thing, and being able to trust in the unfolding of our life.

As a teacher, one of the things I see is the failure of people to trust their lives—their problems and sometimes even their successes. It is a failure to trust that their life is its own teacher, that within the exact way their human life is expressing itself lies the highest wisdom, and that they can access it *if* they can sit still and listen. If they can sink into themselves, their own nobody-ness, and allow difficulty to strip them of their somebody-ness, then they can do away with the masks of their persona. Spiritually speaking, this is exactly what we want: to remove the masks. Sometimes we take them off willingly, sometimes they fall away, and sometimes they are torn off.

Unmasking *is* the spiritual path. It is not about creating new masks—not even spiritual masks. It is not about going from being a worldly person to a spiritual person or trading a spiritual ego for a materialistic ego. It is a matter of authenticity and of the capacity to trust life, even if life has been tremendously tough. It is stopping right where you are and entering profound listening, availability, and openness. If you feel wonderful, you feel wonderful; if you feel lost, you feel lost, but you can trust in being lost. You can do this without talking to yourself about it and without creating a story around it. We must find that capacity to trust ourselves and to trust our life—all of it, whatever it is—because that is what allows the light to shine and revelation to arise.

We see it when we stop and listen, not with our ears and not with our mind, but with our heart, with a tender and intimate quality of awareness that opens us beyond our conditioned ways of experiencing any moment. My first retreat, as difficult as it was, taught me that the most amazing things can come out of the most difficult experiences if we dedicate ourselves to showing up for the situation. That is the heart of meditation and the heart of what it takes to discover who and what we are as we turn away from external things and toward the source of love, the source of wisdom, the source of freedom and happiness within. That is where you will find your most important thing.

The Intersection of
Love and Grace

SPIRITUALITY IN ITS DEEPEST SENSE AWAKENS US TO WHO
WE ARE AND FREES OUR NATURAL HUMAN WAY OF BEING
BENEFICIAL, LOVING, AND KIND PRESENCES IN THE WORLD.

For me, one of the most important things is grace. It comes when we receive an insight, something beautiful, love, an opening, or a revelation about the world. In spiritual terms, we often think of grace in relation to experiences, but sometimes grace is the falling away of something—waking up one day and noticing a burden has been lifted. Spiritual practice opens us to both kinds of grace.

When I contemplate grace, I think of my grandfather Harold. We had a wonderful relationship. He was an extraordinary person, although he did not appear so on the surface. He grew up in extreme poverty but had a buoyant spirit and natural goodness of heart. He's the first true Christian I have ever known. Not that he talked about Christianity much, but it was a huge part of his life, and his behavior embodied Christian virtue in a very natural way. I do not mean to suggest that he was a perfect person or that he did not drive my grandmother crazy at times, but his heart was open and generous.

One of the great joys of my early life was going golfing with my grandfather and his best friend and next-door neighbor of fifty years. John was a heavyset German man with a crewcut, a retired engineer.

My grandfather and John were total opposites. John was uptight and very proper. He had a short fuse and could get angry, yet there was something beautiful about him—he had a good heart. You might not notice it when you first met him, but I saw it in his relationship with my grandfather. The two of them were fantastic friends.

I do not know how John felt about my grandfather bringing me to their golf days. He may have been just putting up with having an eleven- or twelve-year-old kid tagging along, but he treated me well. I loved going golfing with them (although I was and still am a terrible golfer), and my grandfather was thrilled I was there.

My grandfather was not self-conscious. He did things for the sheer joy of doing them, without any consideration (as far as I could see) of what anybody might think. One of his favorite things to do when we went golfing was to hide a loaf of Wonder Bread at the bottom of his bag. Along the course, near a small lake that had ducks in it, he would pull out his bread and toss pieces to the ducks. Before long thirty or fifty ducks would be waddling down the fairway, following my grandfather like the Pied Piper as he threw pieces of bread over his shoulder. It was chaotic as we pulled onto the next green surrounded by a large flock of ducks and geese and watched the other golfers' faces.

As a kid, I thought this was wonderful. John, however, hated it. He would swear under his breath, "Damn, Harold. Do you need to feed the goddamn ducks every time?" He complained, and my grandfather blissfully ignored him and went about feeding the ducks and being happy and buoyant about it. The whole scene was a great consternation to John, because it was not his idea of what proper golf decorum dictated. To follow these two through a golf course was one of the most fun and hilarious things I have ever done in my life.

Being a terrible golfer, I never took long to shank a ball into a creek or lake. When I did, my grandfather would roll up his pants, kick off his shoes, and wade into the water looking for my golf ball and every other golf ball he could retrieve. He would emerge with a big smile on his face and ten or twelve balls in his hands. He'd give me my ball back along with the other ones that he had found. He was so proud! I thought it was delightful to see somebody my grandfather's age enjoying himself, but John was not pleased by yet another breach of proper golf decorum. It is not that my grandfather did not care what John thought—at times I would see him reel it in for John's benefit—but my grandfather was who he was: an open-hearted, open-minded being of great generosity.

My grandfather and I once took a long trip from California up into the middle of Alaska via the Alaska Highway, which was more than a thousand miles of (at the time) dirt road. What an adventure! We drove the better part of each day and then stopped at a campground for the night. After we had set up camp, my grandfather would make his rounds, introducing himself to people and starting conversations. He had an amazing way of connecting with people.

After he retired, his life was about service. He went to prisons and talked to prisoners about his Christian faith, and he delivered food for Meals on Wheels. I could go on and on about things he did. My grandfather shared the kind of love that extends to all beings—a wonderful Christian love. The average person looks at everything through a lens of their own conditioning, yet my grandfather—who also had his own conditioning—was led by his heart. He showed me the impact a single human being can have on the lives of people around them. He was not going to let anyone's opinion get in the way of his expression of love and joy. That was a profound lesson: to be with somebody who was who he was and who accepted everybody else as they were.

My grandfather dedicated his whole life to being a good Christian. For him, Christianity was not dogma; it was a beneficial and loving presence in the world and in people's lives. He had so internalized those deeper values that he became them. He was Christian in a natural and spontaneous way. That was his greatest gift. When you were with him, you had no doubt he accepted and loved you. Spirituality in its deepest sense awakens us to who we are and frees our natural human way of being beneficial, loving, and kind presences in the world.

My grandfather said that he wanted to die on an inflatable raft or boat on an alpine lake high in the Sierra Nevada mountains of California. He loved those mountains, as I do, and he loved to spend time on the water. I do not know where he got the idea of an inflatable raft, but he loved fishing. He had a heart problem from a virus he contracted when he was young and working in the steel mills—hot, dangerous, awful places, especially back in the 1930s and '40s. Because he was poor he could not take a break when he got sick, so he kept working, and the virus attacked and enlarged his heart. He always believed that was what would get him in the end. Sure enough, it did. Sometime in his midseventies, he died on one of his favorite lakes up in the Sierras—*while lying on an inflatable raft!* He had a heart attack and passed away right there on the lake, exactly as he had hoped.

When he died, I did not feel sad or grief stricken. He had lived such a great life—a difficult one at times, but he had lived with joy, and he went out with joy. He was such a buoyant, caring spirit that I was taken up into the inner atmosphere of appreciating that he had been in my life and that I had gotten to experience being with him. Ever since, knowing him has heightened my awareness of the roles we play in each other's lives through the quality of our interaction, how heart-fully we are present, and how we can bring love and grace in action to any given moment—that is the grace my grandfather gave me.

Willingness to Trust
the Unknown

GRACE COMES IN MANY PACKAGES—SOME OF THEM EASY,
LIKE A GIFT, AND SOME DIFFICULT.

"Grace" is a word that is used a lot in spirituality and even outside of spirituality. People talk about their experiences of grace as a breakthrough or sudden realization. The Christian definition of grace is "the gift of unearned merit"—when we feel we receive a gift from the universe or God for a reason that we do not understand. We may not feel we deserve it; the only thing we know is that we did not personally create it. We feel fortunate and blessed. Spiritual awakening itself is grace—a windfall, a godsend. Grace comes in many packages—some of them easy, like a gift, and some difficult.

But as I reflect upon this word—"grace"—it means more than those moments of unearned merit. If we see grace only as that, then we cannot acknowledge the aspect of grace that opens our hearts and minds, making us available to the unfolding of new insight or truth. What opens us to grace is the *movement* of grace. We take the biggest leaps in our development and understanding during difficult times—when we experience the loss of a loved one, friend, job, relationship, or health, when we feel we are being pushed to our edge. These moments rarely feel graceful, but they are the most revelatory. Sometimes, when we seem furthest from grace—from any vital understanding or new perspective that might change us at some fundamental level, when we are on the edge of the unknown and do not know where to go—that is when we have our breakthrough.

That does not mean we *must* be pushed to our edge, as there is no law that says, "The way to become available to grace is by suffering a lot." We can suffer and still have no breakthrough. Some people suffer for a lifetime and never reach a deeper understanding. They are in a state of conditioned resistance, holding on tightly and unwilling to look at life in a fresh way. They have accepted the consensus reality and habituation, even if it is not working and even if it is causing pain. They may be suffering, but at least it is a familiar suffering. Sometimes, for moments of grace to occur, we need to push past that conditioning and meet the intensity of loss, the intensity of confusion, and the intensity of having to deal with something overwhelming—especially if we are resistant. Grace is the willingness to see a pattern as a pattern, to see that something is not working in the way we have been going about life, and to see that we won't be able to think ourselves out of it.

The part of grace that is not often discussed is our participation. Grace is always a gift, but sometimes we must work to receive it. What is our individual response that opens us to grace? It is a willingness to embrace the unknowability of a new way of being and a new way of relating to what is happening. The opportunity arises when you find yourself in a place between a patterned way of being and psychological turmoil and realize that you do not know what to do with the situation. If in that moment you are willing to embrace that insecurity, transformation will occur. Grace will arise. That is why the greatest leaps in our personal and human evolution often happen through some of the most difficult experiences in life. Sometimes we let go because we are desperate. We are tired of suffering, we cannot sustain it a minute longer, and we are willing to let go, even though we have no idea what the outcome will be. The one thing we know is that we are suffering and so we stop resisting. It takes an act of desperation—or an act of faith—to open like that.

That is grace, the willingness to trust the unknown. It is also at the heart of a deep prayer. As many Christian mystics have said, the deepest prayer is not our words—telling God what we want or what we need—but a state of silent listening, waiting for a response to something. Like prayer, meditation in its deepest sense is an act of faith, trust, and letting go of control. It is a desire for an answer to a question or resolution of a difficulty while being willing to *receive* the answer from somewhere. Whether you think of that "somewhere" as God or universal wisdom or some unknown, untapped dimension of your consciousness does not matter. What matters is having trust within the letting go, and it is often desperation that leads to those moments of trust. When we have exhausted the other options, all we have left is to be open, to listen, and to be available. It can take a lot of sorrow, a lot of struggle, and a lot of suffering to get to that simple place of availability.

That is when we can begin to listen instead of reasserting our confusion; we can open to not knowing, which is its own quietness and its own stillness. It is not the stillness of discipline or of effort. It is the stillness of a wisdom that makes us willing to see that something new, something we cannot even imagine, needs to arise within us. It is not something that we create—it is not a three-step plan—but something that intrinsically arises from the depths of our consciousness. When we internalize that—not merely think it or believe it, but start to see the absolute necessity of it—that brings its own listening; our body becomes a sensitive instrument. We are not trying to escape a moment of difficulty or confusion or emotional upheaval, but allowing ourselves to be exactly where we are, on the edge of the unknown and on the edge of the necessity of a new way of being.

As we come into a state of deeper listening and of deeper availability, we are no longer running from what is, from the situation or from the feeling, but opening to it without an agenda. This is not easy—it takes great humility to accept that you cannot solve the unknown—but you *can* enter its domain, that terrain of availability. This is the environment where grace emerges. It seems like it comes out of nowhere, but we must be able to access that nowhere-ness. You can call it what you will. What we label it is not as important as realizing the necessity of being available to it.

Grace is always there. It is not handed out by some guy in the sky with a beard who chooses who gets it and who does not. The only thing that changes is our willingness *to be open* to grace—to not hold on, even to our greatest insights, but to be present to the wisdom and love from which insights come.

An Element of Surprise

THIS MOMENT IS SO AMAZING. YOU CANNOT BELIEVE
HOW EXTRAORDINARY THIS MOMENT IS.

The ways grace can reveal itself are wide and vast. Think of the moment when Moses saw God in the burning bush. This was a moment of tremendous grace. When Moses climbed that mountain, I do not imagine he had any real idea of what he was going to find. Suddenly a great vision of a burning bush appeared, and from that moment on, his life was irrevocably altered. He came down from the mountain bearing a gift—a new vision of life, of reality, and of God. It is the same with the Buddha's awakening beneath the bodhi tree. I do not suppose he sat down and thought, *Today's the day!* Grace has an element of surprise. Because it is unearned, it feels as though something's been bestowed upon us; easy or difficult, we can be available to it, but we cannot directly bring it about.

There are other forms of grace. A friend who has two children talks about how the birth of his first child changed him forever. He had never imagined in his wildest dreams that he could experience the depth and quality of love that he did when that baby was born. It reoriented his life. It was so powerful that before his wife gave birth to their second child, he wondered if he could have the same extraordinary vividness of love. It seemed incomprehensible that it could happen again. That is a real, life-changing grace.

There is the grace that happens when things are not going well at all, when we lean into the unknown and receive something profound. I have found when something does not go the way you imagined it would or wanted it to, if you are truly available to what *is* happening and to the way something *is* going, you can open and respond to grace. The trajectory will begin to improve, and you will turn a corner and find something you had never dreamed of.

Then there are the seldom-acknowledged moments of grace—things like the gift of waking up in the morning (even if some mornings it may not feel like a gift) and taking a breath, stretching your arms, feeling your heart beat. It is an unprovoked grace. It is not happening because of anything you have done, as you have not necessarily merited that your heart is beating and your lungs are breathing and you can feel the palms of your hands. This extraordinary, overwhelming mystery called life is a gift, and all we need to do is receive it.

There is another part of the experience of grace that is not talked about often: what it means to return what has been given. Grace is a two-way street; it is a gift that is received, and it is a gift that seeks to be given. We receive grace only to give grace, and the more we give grace, the more open we are to receiving it. It is like a circle that can complete itself only when we find some way of embodying or expressing our moments of grace. If we do not do this, if we are only consumers of grace, we may spend a lot of time waiting for it, not seeing that to be able to offer grace—our time and attention, a moment of consciousness, of true availability, of heartful and affectionate awareness—is to embody grace.

A gift of grace I'll never forget was given to me by my fourth-grade teacher, Dr. Vogel. He was a wonderful man, and he may have been the first Buddha I ever met. He was truly an enlightened being. That year, we had to give speeches in front of the class. It was supposed to be a one-page speech, no longer and no shorter. When my turn came, I was nervous. I had never done something like this before. I walked to the front of the classroom, put my piece of paper on the lectern, and looked out at the other students. Their eyes were riveted on me. I panicked to such an extent that when I looked down at my speech, I could not make out the words. My mind was so flustered and so shocked by fear that I could not read. This made my panic worse.

I looked up and saw Dr. Vogel at the back of the classroom. He was a roly-poly guy and had his hands folded on his big tummy. He wore the widest, most beatific grin. He smiled with such joy and love that it was a transmission—his consciousness into mine. His sense of okayness reached me, as if he were saying, "Kid, this moment is so amazing. You cannot believe how extraordinary this moment is."

There I was in a total panic, yet his expression was telling me that this moment was perfect. I looked at his face and could feel what he was feeling. I could feel the energy of his confidence come into my body and fill me up like a balloon with air, and when I looked at my piece of paper again, I could read the words. But I did not read that speech. Instead, I looked directly into the eyes of my classmates, and I began to speak spontaneously. I talked for about ten minutes, and it was so easy and delightful that I was over the moon with happiness and well-being.

Ever since that moment, I have been able to speak in front of people, no matter how large the group, with ease and a certain degree of confidence. It is the reason I can do what I do as a spiritual teacher, even though I am a shy person by nature. I owe it to Dr. Vogel in fourth grade. He transmitted grace to me. I can imagine a lot of other adults would feel uncomfortable if they looked up and saw a kid panicking. They would panic for you. Dr. Vogel did not do that. He grinned at me, not because he was trying to help me, but because he knew that *everything was okay*. He knew in the depth of his being that this was a glorious and fantastic moment, and he beamed that truth from the back of the room—a wordless transmission of grace.

I have reflected upon this many times, not only because it was a moment of grace for me, but because he was offering grace—the grace of his certainty of the goodness of that moment and the goodness of me. He had total and absolute confidence in me, even as I panicked. We could all use somebody like that in our lives, couldn't we? Whether we have someone like that or not, we can all find grace within ourselves and become conscious of the way we can be emissaries of grace: humble, not overbearing, and not insisting. We each have our own moments of grace; it is not a spiritual thing, and it is not restricted to moments of revelation, although it includes those. There are many times in life when we may feel graced, and there are endless opportunities to bring forth that grace and offer it to the world around us. In that way, bit by bit, we all become more sane, free, and happy.

The Fundamental Realization

I would like to look at the notion of grace in relationship to a most important thing: to the fundamental realization. I call it "fundamental" because it is the realization of what is and has always been the case. Take reality, for example. It is not something that comes into being at some point in time and then disappears at another point in time, only to come into being again at some later time. Reality is *always and already* real. This is the heart of the fundamental realization. You could call it spiritual awakening, enlightenment, or many different names, but it is experienced as a type of grace.

This fundamental realization is always experienced as a grace because it arises spontaneously. Remember that grace can be defined as *unearned* merit—we cannot bring it into being. This is a tricky notion when we apply it to enlightenment. This does not mean that our actions have no relationship to grace, to spontaneous moments of realization, or to spontaneous moments of revelation. To think this is to misunderstand the nature of reality itself. One of the things that the deep revelation of reality shows us is that everything in all of existence is interconnected. You might say it *inter-is*. What we recognize with the grace of awakening is the fundamental nature of that reality, the fundamental nature of that is-ness.

We come to see that it is no other than our own being and no other than our self. When we bump into that reality, we give it many names—Buddha nature, Christ consciousness, the infinite, spirit. I like "spirit" in this context, because spirit is the nature of each and every experience that we may have. Any moment that we are experiencing anything, including this moment right now, is a manifestation of spirit—and being a manifestation of spirit, it all fits together. To conclude that what we do has no relationship to this realization is false. It is more exact to say that what we do does not *directly* cause a moment of grace or awakening. There is no direct causal relationship between our spiritual pursuits and the arising of self-recognition or of spiritual awakening. However, everything we do contributes *indirectly*, because everything is related to everything else—the reason for any one moment is everything else in the entire cosmos that is happening or ever has happened. This is what I mean when I say everything is interrelated, as everything is participating in the causing of everything else.

If there were a direct causal relationship between our actions, our spiritual practice, and the dawning of spiritual enlightenment, then we could turn these elements into a formula that leads to enlightenment, like two plus two equals four. It is not that simple. Neither is the other dualistic idea that what we do has *no* relationship to awakening—that would mean that everything is not interconnected. What we experience with a deep awakening is that everything participates in the happening of everything else. This is what I mean by "nondirect causal relationship." This phrase is a paradox to the intellect, but from a deeper place—from the wisdom eye of prajna, as we say in Zen—we can see that everything is linked together.

This view of reality comes back to our life and grace. Not just the grace of spiritual awakening, but any moment of grace. Grace is always part of the equation, although sometimes we notice it and sometimes we do not. Everything in each moment is a product of everything else. That does not make any moment special, because *every* moment is a display of spirit. This is what awakening shows us.

When I first stumbled into this view, this state of grace, I was about twenty-five and seeking enlightenment with great vigor and intention.

I sought enlightenment the way I sought a lot of things I wanted—I went after it with determination and hard work. Most of that work was meditation, and with that meditation came a lot of wondering and a lot of inquiry. I was reading a great deal as well, though not so much to collect information as to explore my creative yearning. I did not know what my breakthrough was going to be, but I had an intuitive feeling that there was a different way to perceive myself and life.

One day, when I was in this state of seeking and spending time in meditation, the doors of perception suddenly opened. One of the biggest surprises for me was the already and always nature of reality: I realized the reality that I had been seeking had always been here. And not only had it always been here, but *I was it*. I do not mean "I" as an ego or personality, but "I" as the reality itself that woke up. In one sense, I woke up from myself as I had known myself. That is the amazing thing of it: here we are being ourselves and struggling toward a spiritual breakthrough, when we realize that the person who is trying to have the breakthrough is not separate from spirit. I had been chasing reality or enlightenment, and all the time I was it—I was that reality, and I was that enlightenment.

Can I say that what I was doing—all my meditation practice, seeking, wondering, curiosity, reading, writing, and the rest of it—is what brought about that moment of clarity? Can I take credit for it occurring? In one sense, I cannot, because I did not cause it. You do not bring about reality. However, even though I did not cause it directly, everything I did was a manifestation of awakening and arising into consciousness. We come to spiritual practice because the deeper reality is *already* arising, and the first way it arises into our consciousness is as the spiritual drive itself and as the yearning. Yearning may not be the fruition of enlightenment, it may not be the recognition of enlightenment, but it is the arising of it. If it was not beginning to arise into consciousness, we would not have any yearning at all, and we would not care.

What we do has great impact. It is not the direct cause, it is indirect, but our entire spiritual impulse is the arising of awakened consciousness into our lives. Anybody who has a deep moment of recognition or awakening cannot help but see this. One of the most surprising parts about it all is that here we are seeking something we already were, but we did not know what we were, so we sought as if it was other than us. However, by seeking reality (or Buddha nature, or awakening, or enlightenment) as if it is something other than what we are and something other than what is happening in this moment, we unwittingly avoid it, in the sense that our seeking causes us to not perceive what is already and always the case.

In this very moment, the awareness that is reading these words, the awareness that looks out, the awareness that sees, the awareness that is hearing the sounds around you—recognizing that awareness, before you even try to be aware, is the doorway to the fundamental reality. That awareness *is* the awareness of the infinite; that awareness is itself the infinite being aware.

It is fine to have an awareness practice in which you are trying to be more present to what is happening. That has its place, but I am talking about something different: *not* trying to enhance the quality of your attention, but relaxing into the nature of awareness itself. Then you come to see that everything else is in a constant state of change and you, whatever you are, are always there, whether there is something occurring or not occurring, whether you are having an experience or not, whether you are thinking or not thinking.

What you are is always here, and the only thing that is always here is awareness or consciousness. It is in every experience, and it is in every sight, sound, smell, taste, and sensation. There is no need to try to get rid of anything you see, or smell, or taste, or touch, or recognize. If you are trying to get rid of it, that means you are trying to change objects, which keeps you stuck in the world of objects. For the sake of self-recognition, we should relinquish being stuck on the object of our perception, of our awareness, and allow awareness to sense back into itself. Awareness, when it is sensing back into itself, is an open, spacious, empty, attentive quality.

If you sense into awareness itself at any moment, you might recognize yourself to *be* awareness itself. It is possible that awareness might recognize it is the ground of all experience and that experience is a display of this ultimate ground of being. So everything is the display of spirit, and everything is the display of awareness. These are only words, but hopefully they are words that are pointers, so you begin to sense that it is impossible to relax into the nature of awareness itself and still be seeking, because all seeking will be seeking something to occur within awareness. All seeking is in the future—it is yearning for something that is not present—while with a direct teaching, or a direct pointing to the nature of reality, we are relinquishing the future. We are relinquishing the pursuit of something that might occur at some other time, so that we can sink into the nature of *this* moment. The reason is because the nature of reality is constant. It is always here, so any state will do and any experience will do; there is nothing that is outside of spirit. You do not have to look for a better moment or a better state. As you sink into the current moment, you see that the whole moment is flooded with the light of awareness—the light of consciousness.

If you keep sinking into being awareness, you might begin to sense that what we call "the world" is an idea and is itself an expression of awareness and of spirit. These things come to us by our relaxing into our current awareness. It is as simple as that. If there is a way, that is the way. The desire to sink back into the nature of the current moment, into awareness, is a grace. Where did that desire come from? Where did that willingness come from?

The ultimate grace is to see that each moment is grace; it is its own miracle. When we experience the moment like that, it is a gift. All we ever needed to do was to settle into it and to recognize the nature of our being.

Challenged by the Great Sorrow of the World

IT TAKES A LOT OF FAITH TO SIT DOWN RIGHT
IN THE MIDDLE OF YOUR EXISTENCE.

Difficulty opens us to moments of grace during which we are reminded of the great vitality beneath the surface of things—beneath the way things seem to be. When we even talk about grace or about any moment of breakthrough into a greater sense of the reality of which we are a part and which we are, we think of it as something extraordinarily pleasant or at least more pleasant than the environment we are in. We believe that if we could only separate from our difficulties, if we could not be so challenged by what occurs day to day, we would have a better opportunity for moments of grace to occur; we would be more able to open to a bigger sense of reality and of who we are. It is interesting that we hold these ideas of what is conducive to grace, to spiritual breakthrough, because they actually contradict the moments when grace shows up.

Sometimes we do have moments of grace and deeper understanding when we are in a serene, comfortable, safe environment. Grace can arise as we are walking through the forest on a quiet day when nothing is disturbing us, and we are taken by the great silence and held by that sense of nature that allows us to relax into the greater reality of what we are. However, after more than two decades of teaching, I have found that grace comes more often through great challenges: when we are coming up against some edge in our lives, when we do not know how to handle a situation, or when our normal ways of coping are not useful and we find ourselves on unfamiliar ground. The challenge could be the loss of a loved one or the loss of a job; it could be a serious illness or any manner of things that leave us no choice but to draw upon a capacity within us that we might not know how to access otherwise.

We see this in stories from all the great religious traditions. The Buddha is a good example. He wanted to find out if there was any answer to the existential human dilemma of the unavoidable facts of birth, life, death, and suffering. He was motivated by seeing something we all recognize at some point or another: life holds a great deal of suffering. In his time, if you were going to go on a serious spiritual quest, it was common to become a renunciant, so he left his home, his wife and children, and his princely ease and wealth to seek answers. After six years of arduous spiritual practices and disciplines like fasting and self-mortification, after mastering religious teachings and many styles of meditation, he realized he had to face the truth that he had not found the answer he was seeking.

This was the Buddha's turning point—a period of great despair for him. Imagine you have given up everything in your life to go on a quest and you have done the hard work, you have practiced and studied with the great teachers of the day, yet after years of seeking you realize you have not found what you were looking for. What a disappointment! On top of that, the Buddha was starving to death, because his ascetic practices had worn down his body—he looked like a skeleton. We know the image of the Buddha sitting under the bodhi tree, but we often forget that what got him under the bodhi tree was the pain of meeting his own edge, of being brought to a place within himself that he did not know how to break through. In this difficult moment, he did not know he was approaching that mysterious and powerful dawning of grace that would open a new vista of realization—of connection with life.

The bodhi tree is a mythic motif. The tree stands for the tree of life, much like the tree of immortality in the Qur'an or the tree of knowledge in the book of Genesis in the Bible. Adam and Eve plucked the fruit from the tree. The Buddha did not take anything from the bodhi tree but sat down under it. He sat *with* the stark reality of life. He committed himself to life, but not in the way we usually think of committing ourselves—squeezing it for all the vitality we can. Instead he sat down at the root of existence and tried to find a resolution to the unavoidable fact of human existence, and he woke up. That is why the image of the Buddha under the bodhi tree is a teaching unto itself. When we come to a great barrier, when we find a place inside us we do not know how to navigate, when we are in a painful experience that we cannot avoid, we need to *sit down right there*—at the root of that experience, at the root of the tree of life—and *be still*. It is not an easy teaching, but it is a great teaching: be still amid difficulty, making yourself available to whatever is occurring in that moment.

Being still is not an act of physical motionlessness or of quieting the mind. It is about being available to whatever is occurring in every moment. When we are completely open—even if it is difficult—we have stopped fighting against life, we have stopped moving against whatever situation we find ourselves in, and there is a possibility for discovery. This is where a great movement of grace can occur. We stop trying to run away from what is and sit down right in the middle of it—even if it is unknown—and reach a place of deeper understanding.

It takes a lot of faith to sit down right in the middle of your existence. This is not the same as the "faith" that a doctrine or teaching or teacher is the truth. That is actually a belief, which tells us how to interpret life and find comfort and safety within it; a belief provides a way of insulating ourselves from real faith—from real trust. Faith in its truest sense is something different. Faith allows us to let go of belief, of how we habitually translate each moment of our experience into a conceptual model that seems to make it easier to understand, seems to give us some control, and eases the feeling of insecurity we have whenever we find ourselves on some edge. Your edge could be challenges in your work or relationship; it could be illness or a loved one's death or even your own impending death; it could be your feeling very challenged by the great sorrow of the world. A lot of things can make you feel like you are on an edge and you do not know what to do with it.

This is what happened to Jesus in the Gospels. He lived an engaged, dynamic life. He was not a renunciant, he was not a Buddha, he did not seek out a monastic order—he was a man of the world—but even he had times when he needed to be alone. At the beginning of the story when he's at the Jordan River and he's baptized by John the Baptist, the text says that the heavens opened and the spirit of God descended upon Jesus like a dove. That was the moment of a great spiritual infusion—an awakening. The first thing he did after that was head to the desert, because he felt compelled to be with his aloneness. He may have had the idea that he was going to go out to the desert to bask in the glory of the spirit that descended upon him and marinate in that, but something different happened. Jesus found himself on an edge; he was challenged. In the story of Jesus's life, that is represented by the devil.

The Buddha and Jesus found themselves challenged and had to rise to meet these challenges. In other words, they found grace amid great upheaval. Jesus revisited this challenge and upheaval repeatedly until the end of his life. Even when he was in the Garden of Gethsemane a few days before he was crucified, he knew what was going to happen, and he broke down crying and begged God to "take this cup from my lips." That is a poetic way of saying, "How do I get out of this?" It is a human response, when we are challenged or overwhelmed, to ask or hope to have that obstacle taken away, yet spiritual teachings show us how to meet these moments and what to draw upon. One of the common themes is being willing to not run or try to escape. Even though Jesus asked God if he could somehow get out of his situation, right after he spoke those words he reestablished his inner equilibrium and said, "Thy will be done." It is as if he drew upon his deeper sense of being and accepted his destiny—his edge—even though it was terrifying. Think about it: crucifixion is one of the grisliest ways a person can die, and he knew it would happen.

In the stories of Jesus and of the Buddha, many of the images are dramatized and overstated, but that is so we do not miss the point. These teachings convey something important about finding grace in our challenges. The most difficult moments of life give us a point of access, of possibility to be open to grace that is beyond our ability to create or manufacture. In other words, we can meet the moment with a yes, or we can say no or hesitate, complain, or be afraid because we cannot get past our insecurity. If we can say yes to those experiences, if we do not try to avoid them or explain them away, something deeper will arise in that space where we open to our limitation. That is grace.

I experienced this grace in my father. During the last five years of his life, he had a heart attack, a stroke, and then an advanced cancer that took him within a couple of months after being diagnosed. When he was recovering from the stroke, my father told me he had had a near-death experience that removed the fear of death from him, so it was a great grace in that sense. Yet the stroke was challenging, as he lost a lot of function for a while. A fair amount of it came back over time, but not everything, for he never regained the use of one arm and hand. Nonetheless he said, "My stroke saved my life." This was a wonderful way of communicating what he had experienced. Through the challenge of that stroke, he came alive in a new way. He found something he had always been looking for, which was a real experience of love—not an exterior love, but something deep inside. For the last few years of his life, you could never enter the room he was in without him telling you how much he loved you. He would say this to every-body. He had his moments of challenge, when he was depressed by his situation, coping with a body that did not work the way it used to and a mind that was not as sharp as it had been. However, he exhibited this sense of okay-ness through it all and an appreciation, which he was not slow to bestow upon the people around him.

A stroke is an experience that most people hope will never happen to them, yet although there were great challenges for my father, it was a grace, and it did indeed save his life. It gave him a much deeper appreciation for everybody and everything. During his last months, when he had cancer and was dying, he was ready and willing to let go, and his letting go, when it finally came about, was something of extraordinary beauty. A heart attack, a stroke, and then a massive tumor—his experience of all this was great grace.

If we can discover a radical faith (and sometimes the deepest faith comes out of the deepest despondency or mistrust), if we can meet challenges head on—not try to escape, not play victim, not try to explain things away with complicated theologies or psychologies, but open to that part of life that is unavoidable—then we will be open to grace. If life teaches us anything, it is that we are not in control. Enlightenment allows us to let go of trying to control life and of trying to maximize our advantage. Then we can become available to grace and to a new perspective wherein we find a capacity to embrace life in such a way that we will someday look back on our most challenging experiences and see they were our greatest gifts. The things we are trying to avoid are what lead to awakening and to new and broader ways of seeing and experiencing life—of experiencing ourselves.

May your life continue to open you to moments of revelation.

Vital Moments

REST IN *NOT KNOWING.*

There are times when a great deal depends on the decisions we make and which direction we go in. I call these "vitality moments." Sometimes, when we are in the thick of it, we understand our choices are vital; at other times, these moments are harder to spot. Sometimes we notice important, vital moments only when we look backward, as if in the rearview mirror.

We can explore vitality moments within the context of our spiritual search. If we consider some of the myths of great spiritual beings, there is always a vital moment in the story. The first that comes to mind is the Buddha, who left the life that he knew and his family and became a renunciant in order to seek the answers to his questions about the nature of human existence. When he came into an unfiltered, visceral relationship with suffering, sickness, old age, and death, he saw that this is how everything ends. His was a universal reaction: as we grow up, at a certain age we confront our mortality and accept that one of the few guarantees life offers is death. That is when the Buddha had his vitality moment, or turning point, when he recognized some fundamental aspects of the human experience: that everything is changing and that nothing lasts forever. In one sense, vitality moments are an obvious part of living, yet few people experience them in a deep and profound way. It is as if we notice them enough to try to change our focus, to look away, or to think about something else. That is not what the Buddha did; he dove into that great mystery of the unavoidable and inevitable aspect of life, which is suffering. The Buddha's whole life pivoted on how he responded to this observation.

Divine guidance always arises like a whisper. It does not yell, and it does not insist. It is a quiet thing. We cannot hear the whispers of divine guidance until we have embraced where we are. Let yourself know that and rest with it; realize that sometimes knowing what is not working is extremely important, and you do not need to jump past knowing that you do not know. You can let yourself stop right in the middle of the insecurity.

In the Buddha's story, when he reached that point, the first thing he did was veer from the renunciant path. He found himself by a river, half-emaciated and starving to death. A woman offered him some milk and later some food, which he accepted—a no-no for a holy man at that time. By receiving this woman's compassion in the form of nourishment, he had to relinquish his entire world view about what a spiritual seeker should and should not be doing. He had to let himself step outside of the paradigm, but he did not have a plan. He knew that he had not found what he was looking for. Breaking some of the rules of the renunciant life changed the trajectory—whether he knew it or not—of his whole spiritual search. That was a vital moment!

It was a vital moment not only for him to know what was not working, but also for him to accept help from the woman. It was a vital moment because it was something the Buddha would not have done before. It was a decision that altered his spiritual life. I imagine he did not know that or understand it at the time; rather, he was following a voice of authenticity within himself in a deep way. This led to him sitting under the bodhi tree and making his declaration that he would not move until he reached enlightenment, and the story goes on from there.

Transformation tends to happen when we stop or something stops us—a tragedy, a difficulty—and we reassess and realize that the way we are going about life must be redefined. Sometimes we will need to redefine our whole identity. This does not just happen to spiritually advanced beings—this is human stuff. These moments occur with some regularity, and if we recognize how important they are, when they come, we can see them as both great challenges and great opportunities. How we respond is important. Do we search for a quick solution, for a quick answer, or for somebody to save us from our insecurity? Or do we find the wherewithal to settle into those moments and meet ourselves, like the Buddha did? We can lean forward into what is occurring, into the human experience or unresolved quality—whether it is doubt, or fear, or hesitation, or indecision, or whatever our pattern is that causes us to not throw ourselves entirely into that moment.

We never know when these moments are coming. Some are big, and some are much smaller. We should not assume that the small moments are not as important as the big, obvious ones, because attending to the small moments is the way we build a capacity to attend to the big moments of crisis. It is the reason why most spiritual traditions have various ways of getting us to pay attention to our life, even when nothing significant seems to be going on. This comes from an acknowledgment, a realization that vital moments are current in our life and there are decisions being made—consciously or unconsciously—about how we are going to relate to them.

Do you relate to life as an unfolding mystery and an adventure of discovery? An encounter with your immense capacity for wisdom, love, and experiencing life with intimacy and vitality? We have extraordinary abilities as human beings when we begin to recognize the vitality of certain moments and we bring a consciousness to them. These vitality moments happen in our lives with great regularity and are opportunities for awakening and transformation. We must repeatedly embrace the insecurity of these moments and by doing so come to trust them and so ourselves. In these moments, all we need is knowledge of the next step and the willingness to take it. Paradoxically, the knowing of what the next step is arises when we have the capacity to rest in *not knowing* what the next step is and to recognize this is an intimate part of the process of transformation.

Deep Wisdom
in Uncertainty

MOVE OR FALL.

Vitality moments sometimes come out of the experience of fear. As we all know, there are many varieties of fear, but some aspects of the experience of being afraid, of insecurity, can be revelatory.

I used to do a lot of rock climbing. One time, my climbing partner and I were about 750 feet above ground in the Sierra Nevada mountains of California, scaling a rock face called Lover's Leap. I was leading, which is more dangerous than following. The lead climber is attached to the rope, and they wedge protection devices into cracks and clip the rope onto them. If the lead falls, hopefully whatever they put into that crack will hold the rope, in combination with their climbing partner putting on the mechanical brake in their harness to stop the fall. It is dangerous because the devices you put in can pull out if you do not anchor them well or if you put them in the wrong space. If this happens, you keep falling until you get to one that does not pull out. The thing is, say you climb ten feet above the last protection device. If you fall, you fall those ten feet attached to your slack rope and an added ten feet, at which point the slack rope becomes tight and holds you—making it a twenty-foot fall. Again, this is assuming the protection device holds. When we do some of these more high-risk activities, we put ourselves into positions in which choices are no longer theoretical; we could be severely injured or even die. It is the same with life—we can find ourselves in situations we never thought we would be in.

When I was lead climbing Lover's Leap, I got myself into a difficult position. I was in what is called an off-width crack. It is a crack in the rock that is too wide to jam your hands into in order to pull yourself up, but not wide enough to wedge your legs or upper body in and then climb. I could not figure out how to get beyond it. I stood there on this vertical rock face with my fist jammed into the crack to keep myself from falling, trying to figure out what to do next. As the minutes went by, my arms and my fingers grew fatigued, and I began to try desperately to get beyond this place. My point of protection was about twenty feet below me, so I was looking at a forty-foot fall at best. That is a scary distance, and you can be injured if you swing back and smash into the rock face.

I was up there for a good fifteen minutes trying to get past this one off-width crack. At some point, I realized I had better try to get a piece of protection right in the crack, which I should have done at the beginning. I put a spring-loaded camming device into the crack and tried to pull the rope and clip it into this protection piece. I had become so weak that I could not tug the rope up between my legs; the ropes can be heavy, and they go through lots of other pieces of protection, which puts drag on them.

When I realized I could not pull the rope up and clip it, I knew I was in real trouble. My legs shook, my breathing grew labored, and I recognized I might have another fifteen seconds before I fell out of sheer fatigue. I thought, *I have to move, and I have to move right now. I am going to fall either way, whether I move or not, so I have to try.*

I did, and it was amazing! Within seconds, I had passed the difficult position. I got to a safe little ledge, where I sat down and tied myself in to recover. As I lay there on my back for about five minutes while the adrenaline shook out of my body and my heart rate returned to normal, I thought, *By God, I'll never do this again.* Then I belayed my partner up, and the second half of our climb was delightful. It ended up being a lovely day.

A few things fascinated me in the wake of this. The first was how this was an extreme example of getting ourselves into any predicament in which we do not know where to go. We all find ourselves in situations in which we say, "I cannot seem to go forward. I do not know the move to make." Then fear comes in, and it is easy to become immobilized. Everybody would agree that fear, at least if left unchecked, is overwhelming and seems to blind us to our choices.

When I was on that rock face, I was forced into a predicament in which I had two options: move or fall. Given those options, something in me shifted. It was not my mind that shifted; I did not sit there and figure out the most efficient way to get beyond the off-width crack. My legs were trembling, and I was growing weak. I did not have any time left. I accessed something deeper within myself, but only when I absolutely *had* to access it because I had run out of choices. The only one left was to let go and move. Once I let go, there was no room for hesitation.

Sometimes we are in situations when the moment dictates that we act. I have talked to a lot of people over the years who have told me about being in a real emergency—somebody's life was on the line, someone was injured, something happened that forced them to act decisively and instantly—where the consequences were high, yet there was no time to think about them. They said the action seemed to happen *through* them when they transcended the debilitating effect of fear. Most of us have had those moments, and when we look back, we realize the tremendous consequences that were in play. We are astonished that there is something within us human beings that can act and respond in such an amazing way when we let go of fear. In those moments when we *must* act, we are transcending the self.

The Buddha called that leap from fear to faith, or any best choice for a situation, "right action." This is an action that is spontaneous and not premeditated. It is coming, not from the ego, but from a different place—that dimension of action, of wisdom, of love, and of compassion that is integral to our being. We may or may not have conscious contact with it, but nonetheless it is there. That moment on the rock face taught me that something can occur beyond our mind's ability to understand or predict. There is a resource there, and if we can trust enough, it becomes accessible. On Lover's Leap, I accessed it through real fear for my life in an extreme situation.

What this showed me was that when I ran out of time and I had to act, something almost acted *for* me—something leaped into the situation and did it for me.

In Zen Buddhism, there is a tradition of koan study, of paradoxical questions—like puzzles—teachers give you as a student. The challenge is to come up with a response that is your own.

Koans are an exercise to put you into a psychological state like the one I was in up there on that rock face. They are not necessarily meant to scare you to death, but they are intended to put you in a position where none of your conditioned responses work. You can analyze forever, you can be Einstein, you can be the smartest person in the world, but you cannot think yourself into a resolution. The only way you can resolve a koan is by taking a leap beyond the conceptualizing, conditioned state of mind into something else.

When I was on Lover's Leap, I was presented with a koan called "Saving Your Life." I had run out of potential actions, but I had to do something in that instant. That experience was the beginning of learning a trust that is essential in life. No matter how we come about it, we can trust in something that is beyond our current experience, beyond our current knowledge, and beyond mind. This resource of great wisdom and love, this faith, is rooted within our being. It feels like a grace—it feels like something extraordinary.

This is not something we are taught, so by the time someone talks to us about it, it seems abstract. "I get what you are saying, but I do not quite get *how* to do it. Can you tell me how to go about this?" If I were to create a three-point plan about how to move beyond confusing moments, it would look something like this:

1. *Stop* and feel where you are. Stop struggling to get out, stop looking for security, and stop anxiously reaching for the answer or the resolution.

2. *Feel* the presence of that moment and let yourself inhabit the quieter part of your being by being willing to *not* know and to stay in an insecure, unconcluded inner atmosphere.

3. *Open* to a new vision, to something that is not a repeat
   of the same old way you have done things, which never
   worked. You must be open and listen. If we were to talk
   about it in the old language, we would say, "Listen to
   the whisper of God."

We have become so estranged from this process, so cut off and
housed in this abstract realm of mind, that we have lost touch with our
incredible capacities as human beings to sense and feel. How do you
stop to sense and feel something? That first breath that fills your lungs
on a cold morning and brings you into a deeper state of aliveness, the
breakfast you eat, the coffee that you drink, the feel of the road under
the tires of the car as you drive down the freeway to work—how are
you paying attention to something other than the narrative that is
clamoring in your mind?

If we wait until we find ourselves in a crisis to start to listen, it
is difficult. Being awake and inwardly listening to what we do not
know, sustaining the presence of quiet, insecurity, and nonconclusive-
ness, helps us be in situations in which the conclusions are not easily
grasped. It is a kind of practice. The more we do it, the more sensitive
we become. The body, mind, and senses grow heightened the more we
rely on them, the more we give them time and attention, and the more
we engage them. Start with the small stuff. Sense your way through
inconsequential things, and practice with moments that do not seem
to be that important. Get the feel of what it is like to sustain a sense
of insecurity, to not leap at the quick answer in the conditioned way,
but to listen to a quieter voice and to a whisper inside. Our depth and
wisdom and love exist in the still regions. You will be amazed by what
you can access: the subtler and more refined state of consciousness we
all possess, which is awareness itself.

Life Is a Series of
Unknown Moments

FEAR DOES NOT ALWAYS MEAN DANGER.

Fear is a universal part of the human experience. I do not think any-body gets through a lifetime without moments of fear. One of the things that has struck me over the years is how we relate to fear. There are many kinds of fear generated by physical danger, biologi-cal defenses, our pasts, and our traumas, but here I am interested in exploring the fear of the unknown, because it is one of those fears that lurks, especially for spiritual seekers.

We have all experienced fear of the unknown when we have asked somebody on a first date, or applied for a job, or ventured into any new situation. Spiritual seekers spend a lot of time dwelling in the unknown: when we sit down to meditate and be still, when we are praying and our prayer turns quiet, or when we arrive at a place of mystery. These are times when we do not know what is coming—we are in unknown psychological territory. Fear often arises when people reach this territory, which is why as a spiritual teacher I am often asked, "How do I get rid of fear? How do I deal with it? What do I do with it?" Underneath these questions is a fundamental orientation—a belief that when we feel fear, we need to get rid of it as soon as possible.

However, most of our fears are not about survival, as most of our lives are not in peril. So when we are about to experience something new, we intuit a different state of consciousness and a different state of being, and as much as we may yearn for it, we simultaneously become afraid because *we do not know*. The mind may hold a philosophy or theology or belief about what spiritual awakening is or what it can reveal, but until we have had that awakening, until we have had that revelation, until we have gone through it, we do not know *what it is*, and we do not know what is in store for us. This link between fear and the unknown is both common and profound.

It is funny, because when we are happy, we do not think, *How do I get rid of this happiness as fast as possible?* nor, when we are feeling peace, do we ask, *How do I get rid of this peace as fast as possible?* But when we feel fear, we wonder, *How can I end this fear as fast as possible?* or *How can I avoid this fear?* These are conditioned ways of reacting. I like to tell people, "If you are going to endeavor into a deep form of spirituality, into a deeper practice, you should count on visiting a lot of unknown psychological and spiritual terrain, because that is what most of the spiritual disciplines are meant to introduce you to."

Right before people have meaningful spiritual shifts, the most common thing for them to experience is some variety of fear. It is as if there is a protector at the gateless gate (as we say in Zen) to Nirvana, to enlightenment, and to awakening. Even though there is no barrier—there is nothing holding us back, there is nothing threatening us—we become afraid because the whole landscape of awakening is such a different way of seeing and experiencing life that the intuition of it arising is concurrently thrilling and terrifying. The mind asks, *Well, what* is *going to happen?* and we reflect and realize we have no idea. This is when things get frightening.

Part of engaging in a spiritual life is becoming profoundly conscious, and when we do, we start to recognize the overwhelming amount of unknown in our lives. We need to learn that fear does not always mean actual danger. As human beings, we are conditioned to think that what we know will keep us safe and what we do not know is a potential threat and therefore makes us afraid. It is healthy to reexamine this belief and look at our relationship with fear, because what we imagine we know is worthier of fear than what we do not know. Take death, for example: when people think about death they get afraid, but the thing is, you cannot be afraid of death—you can only be afraid of what you *imagine* death to be. You can imagine death to be annihilation, or you can imagine death to be anything, as there are so many different stories about what is going to happen after we die. Death is the ultimate unknown. So, once again, it is the psychological landscapes where we do not know what will be or what will happen that make us afraid.

We do much more damage to ourselves and others with the things we *think* we know—with our certainty—than we ever do with our uncertainty or with the unknown. A lot of destruction happens when we pretend to know things that we do not know. It is a refusal to embrace the unknown aspects of life, which is just one unknown after another. We do not know what is going to happen one second from now. From the moment we were born, we have never known what was going to happen from one minute to the next. We can be afraid of that, as if it is somehow problematic. What do we do that causes the most danger?

It is not the things we do not know that create danger; it is what we imagine we know. Most wars are the result of what a group of people *imagined* to be true. Even if you have an argument with a friend or a spouse, the argument is usually based on two people *imagining* they know what is right or wrong. Most of the damage we cause to ourselves and others happens when we become attached to an idea, to a belief, or to an opinion, which is not true knowledge at all.

In some way, we have the whole equation backward and upside-down. To begin to embrace the unknown is not dangerous, but to always be running from the unknown is a way of constantly making yourself afraid. Therefore, the best way to deal with fear is to face it. There is nothing new in this idea—if you are running from fear, you become more afraid of whatever you are running from, because whatever you are running from takes on more significance the longer you run from it. If you can stop right in the middle of your fear of whatever unknown terrain you are encountering in your life or in yourself, then the fear has nothing to sustain it. To continue to build and exist even as an emotion or feeling, fear needs you to resist it, to run from it, and to constantly try to negotiate with it. If you face fear—if you *experience* it—then fear does not have anything to move you with.

If you stop to be with it and feel it, you learn that not all fears are the same. You see that fear of the unknown can only exist if you are running *from* the unknown. For instance, statements like "You do not know what is going to happen from one second to the next" or "From the moment you are born, you do not know how your life's going to unfold" make people afraid. Why is this? There is nothing frightening in these statements. They are factual. So why struggle against them? Mostly because we do not stop, we do not meet the situation as it is, and instead we go into imagination. Imagination is where fear thrives; you are imagining what might happen, what could happen, or what is around the corner. It not only generates but also perpetuates the fear response.

What I am describing is the adult version of the scary monsters of childhood. If a child has watched a scary movie, they may wonder if there is a monster in their room. The best thing to do is to comfort them and then take them by the hand and peek underneath the bed together. No monster. Then sometimes the child will say, "Well, maybe it is in the closet." So you go hand in hand and look inside the closet, and you see there is no monster. What we are doing—without saying this to the child—is showing them that the monster exists only in their mind. The way we deal with the monsters in our minds is to meet them, which means we must let ourselves encounter that moment of meeting.

The key is not to think through all the imagined scenarios; the key is to meet the fear itself. As we gain experience with meeting fear, it stops feeling so intimidating, and gradually our mind and body realize that fear is not dangerous. It is not scary that you do not know what is going to happen tomorrow, and it is not scary that you do not know how something is going to work out, because that is the way life is. That stuff is not frightening until you imagine what *might* happen. The projection is the monster.

Again, we have a similar projection about death, which becomes a problem only when we imagine what *might* happen when we die. So even the fear of death ends up being an imagined fear, because it requires our mind to project into the future. However, if you stick with the fact that "I do not know what will happen when I die," and if you experience that not knowing, you will also experience a tremendous release because you are not telling yourself a lie. You are no longer projecting onto death a scenario that scares you, but you are instead staying with the unknown.

As a teacher, this is what I try to do when people ask me questions about fear. First, I recognize how they are scaring themselves with what they are projecting onto the unknown. Then I show them that to clear that fear, they must stop entering imaginary scenarios that may or may not happen. Instead they should face the fear without any projections, without any story, and without any responses like "This is what might happen."

Circling back to spiritual practice, envision that in a real sense *you*, your true nature, is the unknown. When we realize this, then the unknown becomes less frightening. The fear dwells in the separation, when we see ourselves as different, as fundamentally other than life itself, and as other than the unknown. One of the greatest blessings of facing our fears is we realize that in running from them we have been running from our true nature, from what we are in our deepest sense.

When we stand firmly in the unknown parts of life and stand firmly in the face of fear, we realize that fear does nothing to oppose us and is not a threat. It foreshadows newness—something unknown that is about to be perceived or is about to happen. There is nothing unusual in that, because the unknown is a constant. It is an integral part of life and of existence, and therefore it is an integral part of *you* and of what *you* are. Until we can stop and see fear for what it is, we are going to continue to be pushed around by it. When we stop and face fear, when we are completely still and quiet with the raw experience of it, we will see that it cannot hurt us. When we can embrace fear, life and our inner landscape are no longer intimidating because we are no longer opposing or running.

The great lesson that fear can teach us—the wisdom of stopping right in the middle of it—is that fear does not always mean danger. As I mentioned, fear can be a sign of something new or something unknown. Sometimes it points to the dawning of a whole new state of consciousness. Fear in these situations does not necessarily mean there is anything wrong; it is a sign that things are going right and that we are having a direct experience of the unknown. If we are spiritual seekers, that is precisely what we want, because it is in the unknown that we find our potential for awakening and seeing our true nature—*we are the unknown.*

Meeting the Buddha
on the Road

THERE IS NO SECRET ESSENCE THAT IS IMMUNE
TO THE WORLD OF CHANGE.

There are moments in all our lives when something happens or we engage with someone and we recognize it as unusual, outside the normal contours and texture of our life. We may not realize how fundamental that moment will be at the time, but we see it later and it points us toward our most important thing.

Throughout most of my twenties, I spent summers hiking and camping in the Sierra Nevada range. These mountains were a place of great inspiration, great peace, and great stillness. I would fill up my backpack with as much food as I could carry—usually somewhere between ten days' and two weeks' worth—and take off. When I was running out, I would walk back down and find civilization. There I would repack my backpack with provisions, and out I would go again.

One of the things I love about backpacking is the self-reliance aspect; you are taking care of yourself, and you are carrying everything that you need on your back. There is no bed, no heater, no air conditioner, no refrigerator, and no grocery store, so you are directly encountering life as it is, instead of through a prism of creature comforts—the stuff that protects us from the natural way of things. You have to keep your wits about you. Storms can come up at a moment's notice. Sometimes I was caught in severe lightning storms and the whole earth took on an electric charge, which you can see as a blue haze above the ground when you are up above tree line and which—as you can imagine—can be dangerous. This was all part of what I liked: having to confront the elements, meet life on its own terms, and conform to it instead of having it conform to me.

On one of these trips, I was hiking down the John Muir Trail, which goes from Yosemite National Park to Mount Whitney. It is 210 uninterrupted miles, and there is not a single road to cross. As I was hiking, I came down a side path to a wonderful high lake called Florence Lake. At the other end of the lake I could get resupplied, as there was a campground area accessible by car, a café, and a tiny store. Before I left my home I had mailed a big box of food to myself to pick up there, which I did. Then I went back to the other side of the lake, and I hiked into the high mountains.

As I was walking, I came upon an old man with a long, puffy, white-gray beard camped at the side of the trail. He had his tent set up, and his stove was out. It was midmorning on a beautiful, crisp summer day in the Sierras, and there he was at his little campsite. I stopped to chat with him. I asked him how long he had been up there and how he was enjoying himself, and he said, "I thought I'd come up one last time to see God's good handiwork before I pass away."

I said, "Well, how old are you?"

"Oh, I am eighty-five years old."

This impressed me right from the get-go—at eighty-five years of age, he had put a backpack on his shoulders and was hiking up into the high mountains. He had a twinkle in his eye, something slightly mischievous that got my attention. I pulled up a log and sat down next to him, and we chatted for a while. When he saw the Buddhist mala I wore on my wrist, he said, "What is that?"

I replied, "Oh, it is a Buddhist mala, like a rosary."

Before I could say any more, he said, "Oh, Buddha was an ass," which got my attention because at that time, in my midtwenties, Zen Buddhism was my path of choice. I was a committed Buddhist, and I had my little mala that I wore all the time. Then I meet this delightful old guy in the mountains, and he promptly tells me that Buddha was an ass! A lot of people could have said the same thing and I would have discounted it, but the way he said it was with no anger and no judgment. It was a statement that he left to hang in the air; he did not say anything after it, but he did look at me to see how I would respond.

The first reaction I had was, "Oh? Why do you say that?"

He went on to talk to me about Buddhism, and Christianity, and being in the mountains, and all sorts of things, and we sat there and chatted for the next half hour or forty minutes. Despite his statement that Buddha was an ass, he was a delightful guy. I did not know at the time that he had planted a seed with his words, but my encounter with that old man in the Sierra Nevada mountains stuck with me.

When we were finished chatting and I figured I needed to get on my way, I lifted my backpack and wished him the best. We said our good-byes, and on I went, but what he had said about the Buddha stayed in my mind. It was not even so much what he had said but the way he had said it, with that mischievous glint in his eye. I walked down the trail, contemplating, *Hmm, I wonder why he said that?* It was this seed that was planted into my consciousness.

Fast-forward a couple of years. I was working at a bike shop as a mechanic, and I was wrenching on bikes. I still had my Buddhist mala around my wrist. One day, I had a bike up in the bike stand, and I was working away. I turned to move a few steps, and that mala caught on the stand. Some piece of metal pulled underneath it, and because I was already in motion, it broke the mala, and beads flew all over the place. It was like they exploded off my wrist and bounced all over the floor, went under tables, and were gone forever. I almost burst out laughing. What I was laughing at was that at that moment, my spiritualized ego identity had broken apart, and it was as if it was falling to the floor like those beads, and I was delighted by it.

I bent down and picked up each bead that I could find and put them all in my pocket with the intention of stringing the mala back together. When I was done, I realized that that spiritual identity was over and that I did not need to see myself through the lens of spiritual identification anymore. After I got home and I was looking at those beads, contemplating whether to make them back into a mala—I had made this one by hand in the first place—it was clear to me that it was over. My identity as anything—as a Buddhist, as a Christian—had spilled down onto the floor when that string broke. That is when I recalled what that old man in the mountains had said—but remember, it was not *what* he had said about the Buddha; rather, it was the *way* he had said it, with a glint in his eye, as if he was trying to show me something that I was almost ready to see, but not quite yet. I realized in that moment that this breaking of the mala and the beads scattering all over the floor was somehow a symbolic event. It was like a representation of a shift in consciousness that was happening and that I was not even aware of until it happened. It was a physical representation of my spiritual identity falling away or falling apart—sometimes it is hard to tell the difference.

This did not mean I stopped practicing Buddhism; I kept doing the same things that I always did. I would work with my teacher on weekends and do all the practices, so it is not like any of that changed, but what was missing now was me seeing myself as a Buddhist or as anything else. When that mala snapped, it was like something in my consciousness broke, in a good sense. I had broken my ability to find in a group a spiritual identity, religious identity, or anything else, and that was such a transformative moment. When these internal events occur, the external world seems to mimic what is happening inside of you, and it seems to act as a mirror to your state of being.

I can look back now and see how significant that was. I knew it was important at the time, but I did not know how very much so. I did not have a huge revelation, because this was not about reaching something, but about spiritual or religious identity falling away. I did not yet understand that this too was part of a spiritual undertaking, that it was part of the path. No matter how we construct our identity, whatever we construct it around will eventually be taken away from us when we breathe our last breath on this earth. A big part of the spiritual path is seeing through identities. When we think of identity we may call it "ego identity" or "identity with our past" or "identity with our mind"—with our thoughts and memories—but there are other kinds of identities that are subtler and also more pervasive. There are identities we may not even know that we have until we do not have them anymore.

We can find our identities in almost any way—through our minds, histories, conditioning, education, and religious or political affiliation. When we break them, it is not necessarily because we no longer have any affiliation with a religion or a political point of view; it is that we can have those affiliations without them becoming who we are and without them being felt as identities. You know the joke about how if you want to ruin a party, start talking about politics or religion? Why is it that people can get so upset when someone challenges their political identity or their religious identity? That old man up in the Sierra Nevadas challenged me when I said my mala was a Buddhist rosary by responding, "Oh, Buddha was an ass," with a smile on his face and a glint in his eye.

He was not trying to show me what he thought about the Buddha. It was not about that; it was something else. I sensed his real message as, "Hey, kid, I am trying to show you something here. Do you want to see it?" He—whether he intended to do so or not—had begun the process of severing my spiritual identity, and the moment when the thread that held all the beads together finally broke and the whole thing fell on the floor was when I knew that I had lost my grasping of my Buddhist identity.

I see both of those moments—the broken mala and the man on the trail—as tremendous blessings. I could have been upset with the old guy for what he said about the Buddha, and I could have been distraught that the Buddhist rosary I wore around my wrist every day for years broke and scattered beads all over the floor, but for some reason I was ready for both of those encounters with life. They showed me how to stop finding my identity through my affiliations—in this case, religious affiliation.

It made me see how I had unknowingly constructed a sense of "me," a sense of self, around this label of "Buddhist." How tricky it is the way the egoic mind, the egoic instinct, will take anything and quietly start to weave an identity and a sense of self around it. At the same time as I was trying to see through or go beyond these false identities, the ego mind was creating a new identity—this time as a Buddhist. You can be a Buddhist or a Christian, a Muslim or a Jew without having an identity wrapped around it, and that is what I was left with when these two events finally played out. It was what I call "a foretaste of a deeper revelation or a deeper truth" and a moment when I could feel and sense what it was like not to have a spiritual identity. It was light and spacious and such a relief, because I could do all the things I had been doing—all the Buddhist practices I had engaged in before—but I did not need to create an identity around them.

We all have these things, don't we? We have our religious or spiritual affiliations, our inclinations, and our political points of view; we define ourselves through family, friends, being husbands or wives or parents, whatever our title might be at work, and whatever roles we might play in life. When we look at it, we can see that all these things are perfectly fine to have, as we all have different functions and various roles in this world. Yet it is so easy for the mind to construct a sense of self around them. People unknowingly construct an identity out of these affiliations or points of view, and so when they are challenged, they feel emotionally like their whole being is challenged. That is why politics and religion are such volatile things to talk about. When we are ready, then we can see that we can perform all these functions, all these roles—and with great dedication when necessary—without creating an identity around them.

One of the Buddha's primary teachings was the teaching of "no self." People think that what he meant was no ego, but he did not mean no ego. "No self" means something far more profound. Within the context of how he used the word "self," you could also interpret it in a theistic manner to mean something like "soul." The Buddha was saying there is no secret essence that is immune to the world of change, and there is no unchanging pseudoentity parked behind your eyes that moves on when your body ceases to function. This was what he brought to the world that was truly new. Isn't it ironic that as a practitioner of a religion that has this as one of its fundamental tenets, I was unknowingly using the religion to create and hold on to a new identity?

When I look back at it now, it is almost laughable, but at the time (at least for a while) I was so serious about it. We do tend to like our new identities, whatever they are, until we see through them all and begin to realize we do not need to be grasping them anymore. We do not need to create an identity around the things we love or the things we hate; what we are is something much more mercurial than that. We cannot be limited to any of these conceptual boxes that we keep trying to stuff ourselves into.

These little moments—the old man out on the mountains and the mala breaking—ushered in a whole new phase of my spiritual life. I recognized what was happening, but, as I said, I did not recognize the full significance of it at first. That would take years. We do have these little moments if we care to notice, but if we are too caught up within ourselves and if we are protecting our identities too tightly, we will not see what that moment is trying to show us. We will go into reaction, we will go into protection, and we will oppose the moment when it does not conform to our ideas.

The spiritual life is about seeing through those identities and also seeing how the mind creates new ones as fast as old ones drop away. It is useful to pay attention to the subtle moments in life, because they can act as mirrors for what is going on deep, deep down in our consciousness at a level that we may not be aware of. In this case what the mirror was showing me was: *You do not need that. You do not need to create an identity as a Buddhist or Christian or Jew or Muslim or anything. You do not need to make it into this concrete thing that you identify with.*

Life is a mirror reflecting us every time we protect a sacred idea, affiliation, or point of view. The reason we are usually protecting that or pushing back against someone or something that challenges it is because at those times we feel like they are challenging our very self—and they are. They are challenging how our mind has wrapped itself around an idea or affiliation or point of view and is creating an identity out of it. Life does not care what we form our identity around, and it has no respect for whatever we identify ourselves with—it is going to be what it is. It is as if our identities are bowling balls and pins that come crashing against each other whenever someone is not supporting the person we imagine that we are or when life is unfolding in a manner that seems to challenge the way we have it all figured out.

We all know that big life events—divorce, or a death in the family, or terminal illness, or other crises—can turn our world upside down and, if we are ready for it, turn our sense of self upside down and show it to be what it is: something flimsy that does not hold up to deep introspection or deep analysis. However, it is not only the sudden big moments that can act as subtle liberating mirrors for us. It is through the accrual of small moments, if we have the willingness to pay attention, that we find our day-to-day life is our most direct teacher.

I look back at that old man in the mountains with great fondness and gratitude because he played a part in freeing me from a fixed identity at that time. I also look back with great fondness at the moment of snagging my Buddhist mala on my work stand and having it break and scatter beads all over the bike shop, because that was the moment that my old religious or spiritual identity came apart. I could have been upset with the old guy or been resistant to him; I could have thought that my mala breaking—the mala I had made myself and worn around my wrist for years—was some tragedy. However, for some reason that I cannot take credit for, I was ready for both moments, and so they could each act as teachings. Because I did not resist them and I did not push them away, they had the effect of lightening the load that I was carrying at the time.

These reflecting moments are not rare. They happen every day. The invitation is constantly there, and we can always check in and ask: *Is it necessary to resist this? Is it necessary to resist when someone says they do not agree with us? Is it necessary to resist life when it goes a way that is different than what we had in mind? When we do resist it, what sense of self or what identity are we keeping intact and holding together? Is that necessary? Is that what we want to do? Does that grasping actually free us?*

Every time we grasp, we are limiting our perception and limiting our experience of being. I would encourage you to look at whatever life is mirroring back at you and instead of trying to be something different or better, ask these questions: *Do I need a new fixation? Do I need to make an identity around my interest or my point of view? Can I have it without creating a sense of self? Can I experience a greater freedom by letting go of all the ways I construct identity around my affiliations and the roles that I play in life?* We can all be more awake to what each moment of life is trying to show us, because a willingness to see is all we ever need.

The Dirty Little Secret
of Spiritual Practice

AWAKENING IS ABOUT LETTING GO
OF HOW WE PERCEIVE OUR WORLD.

The dirty little secret of spiritual practice is that confronting the true nature of our self can be terrifying. For those of us who engage in spiritual practice, it is common to struggle with facing our existential fear. This is not the kind of fear that is necessarily derived from the past or from a traumatic event; it comes from a place inside of us. It is that sense within consciousness that we have met an immensity of the unknown or the infinite, and in our fear, we grasp onto our egos.

Ego, broadly speaking, manifests in three parts of our being: conceptual, emotional, and rudimentary. We experience conceptual ego in the mind as images, ideas, beliefs, and judgments. It is intellectualized. When we wake up from that conceptualized ego, our sense of self is no longer found within the matrix of thinking—it is no longer found in what we have been taught or in an image of what we believe. Letting go of conceptual ego is like waking up from a dream; we no longer identify with what we "know" to be true.

The second, more interior form of ego—emotional ego—is held and felt within our chests. I think of it as the North Pole of our ego compass, for when we connect to emotional ego, we feel oriented and like our true selves. However, this is not always something positive;

some egos feel most normal when they are in a negative state—angry, anxious, or ashamed, whatever part of the spectrum of emotional experience is most familiar. We may have woken up from the conceptual ego, but we can still get stuck in the emotional. When we can realize that "I am not those feelings," we will release from the emotional identification with the self. When we do this, there is a freedom from all types of emotional ego: positive, negative, and neutral.

The conceptual and emotional ego orbit around the third part of ego, which is the deepest—what I call "rudimentary ego," rooted down in our belly. If it had language, the language would be a great, big, cosmic "*No!* No to life, no to death, no, no, no . . ." We can be in a state in which we're experiencing no real threat at all, but if we bump into this core level of ego as we're meditating, we may feel an irrational sense that our self will be annihilated. This is the place of existential fear. It is not a fear of death, it is not the fear of getting hurt, but it is the fear of annihilation, of nonexistence, and of not being. When people connect to this fear and talk to me about it—especially of the existential immensity of the infinite or terror of the unknown—they often unconsciously put their hand on the lower part of their belly, because that is the place in the body from which the fear is generated and where it's felt.

The idea of letting go of that contracted, rudimentary fear can seem dangerous. Envision your rudimentary ego like a clenched fist of self. If you imagine a hand making a fist and then releasing it, the fist has been annihilated. At the gut level, this ego is the experience of a contracted void, or a contracted state of emptiness. For this contraction to give way, so that we may be free and know God, we must access something deeper and more fundamental than instinct. In Zen, this is called "the gateless gate" that we pass through as we reach spiritual milestones or shifts. It is "gateless" because all that is happening is that contractions are released, as there was never anything there to begin with—we created the gate in our minds—and we will be annihilated, but not in the way we fear we might. Once we have passed through the gateless gate, once we have unclenched the fist of rudimentary ego, we can access something deeper than instinct and go beyond existential fear.

We can have a million and one spiritual experiences and still hold our egoic identity intact, but when we truly awaken, we transcend at least part of the ego structure. However, that does not mean that it won't reformulate itself and manifest in a new way. Sometimes it does; sometimes it does not. Moving past our existential fears is about seeing through this deep aspect of ego, freeing our consciousness to connect with its own infinity, emptiness, void nature, and nothingness.

Letting go of the ideas held in the mind and the emotions held in the heart is one thing, as we know this does not mean we will never think or feel again. But we can awaken on both these levels and still have our gut rudimentary ego intact, and this existential level of self can keep us in a place of fear. What happens if we unclench the fist of the ego and the self? Some people are afraid they will go crazy—it is a dread of loss of control. It is not a good idea to push through that kind of fear; it is most wisely dealt with when there is a sense of readiness. As our spiritual practice develops, however, we come to recognize that the only thing that will be annihilated is our clinging to the self, we learn to access the deeper place, and it feels good to let go. We realize this clench of fear was a gateless gate and a contraction within consciousness.

Imagine the rudimentary ego structure as a contracted fist again: as it is released, nothing is lost, because there was not anything there to begin with. The ego was contracted consciousness, that is all, so nothing is gained or missing. Only once we have passed through this gateless gate can we understand ego was not a thing to begin with; it was a nightmare of consciousness generated by our mind. The devouring void, the nothingness, and the feeling of impending annihilation have no tangible reality when we unclench the fist and uproot the structure of self—when we wake up.

But even though we may have woken up from our ego dream and seen the other side of the gate past ego and resultant fear, the self is still there waiting for us to come back from our transcendent vacation. That is why we must uproot ego from the core of consciousness. Moving beyond ego rarely happens in a first awakening experience—it takes time and practice—but the more levels of ego we see through, the more we find. They may be easier to deal with when we see ourselves as outside them and as not being defined by them, but nonetheless, a deep and powerful spiritual awakening does not automatically mean that the ego is eliminated.

At the beginning of this chapter, I called this experience of being stuck in a place of fear of annihilation "the dirty little secret of spiritual practice." It is a dirty little secret because it is not discussed openly, even though it is a common experience. Whenever I talk about it, people inevitably respond with, "Oh, my gosh! I am glad you mentioned that. That fear is happening to me!" It is not a good sales pitch to mention that the enlightenment part of the divine journey might include going through existential terror or facing annihilation. That is not something you put on a book cover to attract people, but the truth is, it is part of most people's experience.

Uprooting the ego structure is the end of its world and the end of perceiving life through that psychological mechanism. Afterward, we do not encounter reality the same way, we do not see self the same way, and we do not see others the same way. Things are different, even though nothing has changed—it is the exact same world with all of us bumbling around in it. Awakening is about letting go of how we perceive our world. What we realize—what we get in return—makes what we have lost seem like nothing. Most of what we lose is what led to suffering in the first place. So even though we can call it a loss, it is not one we are going to lament. The good news is there is nothing to be afraid of.

Willingness to Encounter Silence

TO LEAVE ALL OF EXPERIENCE TO ITSELF IS MEDITATION.

Meditation is most often approached in terms of technique—what we do when we meditate. There are countless variations, and anybody who wants to know how to meditate can find instruction in my other books or in lots of places. But what is meditation, really? What is the meditative mind? What is happening when we enter the meditative mind in an authentic way?

One of the first and most powerful aspects of meditation we encounter is its honesty: we are sitting down and facing ourselves. When you are in a quiet space free of external disturbances, like the television or conversation, you are alone with yourself. You can have all sorts of fancy spiritual ideas—we all do—but when you are sitting still and being quiet, it is like gazing in a mirror: you are seeing yourself. When we meditate, what we are doing (at least initially) is noticing the contents of our mind and of our consciousness.

Coming to see the nature of our mind is the aim of meditation, but it is also one of the unsettling things about the practice. We harbor the illusion that we direct our lives and minds, control how we feel and think, until we sit down to face ourselves in silence. This can be humbling, because most human beings do not know how active, uncontrollable, turbulent, and unpredictable the mind is until they take up meditation. Most of the time, the mind is generating thoughts of little or no importance; it is as if your mind is entertaining itself. When the average person walks down the sidewalk, you cannot see their lips moving, but odds are they are having an internal conversation with themselves, as if there were two of them—one talking and the other listening. There cannot be two of anyone, but it feels like that when we are lost in the internal dialogue.

Most forms of meditation are a way of helping us focus awareness on something other than the normal, chaotic state of mind. We enter it in a state of innocence, then we see we have a mind that is noisy—the first layer of conflict—and then our mind is telling us that it should not be so noisy, which creates its own secondary layer of conflict. The first time I ever meditated, I had no idea what was supposed to be happening or not happening. Because I had no idea, I was not adding on to that secondary layer of conflict, which is trying to get beyond the first layer of conflict—what is already there in the mind and the body.

Meditation is an attempt to connect with a deep part of our being that is not defined by the narration of the mind. Nor is it defined by the turbulent emotional waters that one sometimes meets in meditation. In its deepest sense, meditation is an encounter with the silence of your being. This is the heart of meditation: it is a willingness to be with silence.

Silence is not a big part of our cultural conversation. Instead, we are sold ever-better ways of distracting ourselves and convinced that we cannot do without our gadgets. Notwithstanding the practical uses, technology can become another means of creating chaos and disruption. If we are on social media, the room around us may be quiet, but we are not in a place of silence.

Silence can be disquieting for a lot of us. It can feel strange if you are not used to it, which is ironic, because so much of the activity of nature—of which we are a part—occurs in silence. That is why people like to go for a walk in the woods or somewhere else where they can get away from the hustle and noise of human life: it is a way of entering silence. Meditation is a focused way of doing this. The challenge is that when you start to pay attention to the silence within, that is when you hear the noise, and that is where many people engage in a subtle or overt battle with the chaos of the conceptual mind and with the images of the past or future. However, meditation has nothing whatsoever to do with controlling your mind. As a teacher of mine once told me, "If you go to war with your mind, you will be at war forever." What would it mean *not* to be at war with our minds, with our feelings, and with ourselves?

If you are not careful, meditation can become a spiritual competition—not with someone else, but between the desire to be still and the movement of mind. To be in competition is not meditation. To try to constrain all the disparate thoughts in your mind through concentration is not meditation; it is concentration. Meditation is a deep state of listening. That is the heart of it: listening to the quiet places, but as you do so, trying not to assert your will or make your mind conform to a certain pattern, whether to quiet it or to force thinking or not thinking along certain lines.

In meditation, what you are doing is letting go of all forms of conflict and allowing every single part of experience and every single perception to be exactly as it is, because it already is right. We feel the way we feel, we think the way we think, and our internal environment is the way it is in any given moment, so we might as well come into alignment with it. In that sense, meditation runs against the grain. Sometimes we think, *If I could figure my problem out, then I would not have a problem.* But sometimes trying to figure out your problem is creating another problem. To listen to the quiet spaces inside, you must allow every part of your experience to be the way it is. If you do not, then you are in some form of conflict with it, attempting to control how you think or feel. Meditation is the relinquishing of control, not the perfecting of control.

Try looking at it from a subjective point of view: a thought arises and then passes as if floating down a stream. If we are focused on the stream or whether there are thoughts or are not thoughts, then we are engaging in controlled, willful thinking. "Willful thinking" means intentionally engaging the process of thinking. There is a time to do that, but meditation is not that time.

The depth of your meditation depends on your capacity to listen, and most people are not listening when they meditate. They get stuck in whatever technique they are using, caught up in trying to meditate correctly or what they imagine to be correctly, and trying to quiet their mind. There is an unspoken, sometimes unacknowledged agenda that you can carry into meditation, and if you are not careful, that agenda will *become* your meditation. In other words, you will be meditating on your agenda, whether that agenda is for a quiet mind, or to be at peace, or to feel bliss, or whatever it may be. Meditation is the relinquishing of agenda. It is the natural rhythm of thought when you are not consciously adding to it or trying to take anything away from it, when you are not trying to make it happen or stop it from happening.

There is a soft quality to meditation, a fluid quality, because your experience is constantly changing. It is all movement; if you try to stop the fluidity, you go against the natural flow of consciousness. In this sense meditation is about nonopposition, as it is the most subjective form of practicing nonviolence and noninterference. When you are trying to change things, or trying to stop something from happening, or chasing after what you hope will happen, that is a subtle form of violence or control. Meditation is the relinquishing of that attitude, and you cannot let go of what you do not acknowledge. So first acknowledge any desire to control and any conditional effort to control; see it and watch it play out.

Meditation is seeing all of this. It is coming to know the nature of your mind and experiencing when your mind tries to dominate itself, when there is a thought that says, *I must stop thinking*, which is itself a thought; it is seeing thought as thought. It is not necessarily evaluating thought, it is not measuring thought or distinguishing the good from the bad or the useful from the useless, as that is for another time. Meditation is about seeing the whole nature of experience. As you watch your mind, you start to see that trying to control it tends to add conflict, and being too rigid about it sets up an even deeper groove of rigidity in your mind and in your body.

When the watching of the mind grows profound, what Buddhists call "one pointed," then the quality of our awareness begins to allow us to access a deeper state of consciousness and a deeper state of silence. In essence, meditation is like getting into an elevator and taking it to the ground floor; it is a sinking down into your conscious experience of being. We do not have to know how to make it happen, because there is no "how." It is not what we do that allows us to access great depth in meditation. It is as much what we do not do and what we let go of doing. Meditation is the art of letting go of doing.

The first thing people ask when I talk about meditation is, "Well, how do I meditate? What am I supposed to be doing?" That is an understandable question, but meditation is an entering into the unknown. The egoic self or the false self is predicated and built upon what one knows or what one thinks they know—the self that we imagine ourselves to be. But the unknown self is that dimension of being that we cannot know in the normal way; it is not a thought, it is not an image, it is not a belief, it is not a preference, and it has no history. This is what meditation can begin to uncover with a deep state of listening.

If we listen to our thoughts, then we stay in the world of the known, but when we see meditation more as an act of listening to the quiet places inside, then we are letting go of the known. Knowing who we are, knowing what is supposed to happen in meditation, knowing if we are good or bad or right or wrong or skilled or unskilled at meditation—all of that exists in thought. Meditation is letting consciousness, awareness, sink into the unknown and into that which is not speaking. It is not the thoughts that are problematic, it is the attachment to the thoughts. When we try to get rid of our thoughts, we are actually displaying an intense attachment to the thoughts we are trying to get rid of, because the idea that thinks we should get rid of our thoughts exists only within thought.

All of this is meditation. Through watching your own mind and watching your own conscious experience, you begin to access a level of being deeper than anything your mind or thoughts could create. It's a profound and beautiful dimension of consciousness and an experience of self that is not defined by all the old notions of self—beliefs, opinions, preferences, emotions, and the feelings they generate—but is, instead, far beyond that. Leave thought to itself—do not try to get rid of it and do not indulge it. When you think it should be quiet, then it bothers you. When you leave it alone, it won't bother you. To leave all of experience to itself is meditation.

I invite you to take a day and listen. Even when you are not meditating, focus on listening. When you are driving, listen—nothing but that. If your mind talks nonsense, listen; do not add anything to it and do not try to control it, just listen. If you feel something, feel it, but do nothing else. Just feel it, which is another form of listening. At any moment, you can experience that moment and listen, be, and access a much deeper sense of being. Feel the great silence that is always an aspect of listening. One of the things you will hear is silence—and not a silence that is controlled, not a silence that is manufactured by will or by struggle, but one that is a part of consciousness and that presents itself through the act of listening to all the senses.

The meditative mind is extraordinarily sensitive. As useful as thought is, too much makes the mind dull. It needs to be renewed primarily through silence. So take this day to make some room for listening to the quiet spaces inside. Do not make it a goal; just notice what you notice through listening and through being available to what is occurring in each moment of experience. If you do, your experience will take on transparency—it will not feel as heavy and solid, but will start to feel translucent and ephemeral, which allows even more depth. Listen and make room for the deeper dimensions of your being to arise into your consciousness. This is a way to authentically enter a place of meditation.

The Heart of
Contemplation

OUR TRUE NATURE IS THAT WHICH HAS NO OPPOSITE.

Thomas Merton, the twentieth-century Trappist monk and theologian, wrote in *New Seeds of Contemplation*: "Contemplation is precisely the awareness that this 'I' is really 'not I' and the awakening of the unknown 'I' that is beyond observation and reflection and is incapable of commenting upon itself."

That is a sentence worth repeating: "Contemplation is precisely the awareness that this 'I' is really 'not I' and the awakening of the unknown 'I' that is beyond observation and reflection and is incapable of commenting upon itself." The "I" that is familiar to most folks is the "I" we name a hundred times a day: "I am going to work. I am having lunch. I am going to dinner. I am reading this book." This is what Merton is calling "not I." The you that you have come to know through your memory, judgments of good, bad, right, or wrong, your opinions, belief system, and identification with a nationality, race, or gender—all these ways you define yourself—are not you.

What Merton is saying is that contemplation is exactly the aware-ness that this I, the old familiar self that you may have defined yourself as for most of your life, is not your real self at all. The I you have learned, the I that has been put together through the accumulation of thought and memory and image, is a false self. The false self is a continuously moving stream of conditioned thinking, and that conditioned thinking—or a good part of it—will give rise to certain feelings, so those are conditioned feelings as well. The beginning of contemplation, of depth, and of insight is to see that the false self is indeed false. Not "false" meaning bad or wrong, but "false" in the sense that it is not real. It is thoughts that are referring to more thoughts, conclusions that are referring to still more conclusions, and self-images that refer to more images; in other words, it is thinking that does not refer to anything except more self-generated thinking. It is a self-confirming loop: one thought confirms the next thought, which confirms the next and the next, and since all the thoughts are part of the body, there is feeling as well. Thinking something and then feeling it are the two reference points for most human beings: *If I think it and I feel it, then it is real.* But it does not take much reflection to acknowledge we have all thought and felt things to be true that we later found out were not.

Insight is the awareness that this is not the real I and the awakening of the unknown I. Merton makes an interesting choice of words: "the unknown 'I' that is beyond observation and reflection and is incapable of commenting upon itself." It is worth breaking into increments. The true I—what Merton called "the unknown 'I'" (if we want to call it an "I" or "self" at all)—is unknown because it is not a thought, it is not a feeling, it is not an image you could make in your mind, and it is not constructed out of memory. In other words, it is not known in the usual way that we come to know things. The true I is beyond observation and reflection, as Merton says, because it is observing itself.

We can reflect only upon the false self, and we can observe only the false self; we cannot observe the true self, nor can we reflect upon it, at least in the conventional sense of reflecting upon ideas and images. The false self is a waking dream. When you wake up from sleep in the morning, the ego or false self wakes right up with you, and that is the self Merton is asking us to look at. It is a bunch of thoughts, but it is not what you are. The mind frets, *Well, where am I going to find what I am? Where is the truth of my being? Where is my true self?* The mind looks for the true self and looks for the truth as an object—something that awareness can reach out and grasp—but the true self casts no reflection, so it cannot be made into an image and thereby conceived as an object. In the direct perception of our true nature, it is the self-reflective aspect of mind that gives way.

That is why Merton spoke of the unknown I, the unknown self, and the unknown you. Unknown because the true you can never be made into an object of observation—it *is* the observation. It cannot be made into an object arising within consciousness, because true nature is something more akin with the consciousness that is doing the looking. That consciousness—the consciousness that is reading these words, for instance, that is seeing whatever you are seeing and hearing what you are hearing—has no shape and no form. In that sense, it is unknown. It is not unknown in the sense of not being there, and it is not unknown in the sense of being hidden, but it is not something tangible. It is what watches you attempt to reach out and grasp it, so all the grasping for awareness happens within awareness.

Merton was pointing to this when he used this wonderful language: "the unknown 'I' that is beyond observation and reflection and is incapable of commenting upon itself." Incapable of commenting, or of saying that it is good, or bad, or right, or wrong, or talented, or untalented, or male, or female. The true self—if we want to call it a "self" at all—cannot be known in that way, because, although those are labels that we stamp upon ourselves, we exist with or without those labels. Those labels do not define us; they define the false self. All our evaluating defines is the false self, and all our self-judgment defines is the false self, so the false self is nothing but those judgments and evaluations. The unknown self is the self that is not talking back to you, the self that is not found in labels, evaluations, judgments, opinions, or even belief systems—all of which exist within your consciousness.

Merton calls it "the unknown 'I'" and is not making any positive statements about true nature. There is a wisdom in that, because as soon as we define true nature by a positive statement, like, "Oh, okay, it is awareness, and it is consciousness," then it becomes another object within consciousness. Even our idea of consciousness is an idea that arises within consciousness, but the true nature of that consciousness *transcends* the idea. We know this because you can have an idea of consciousness or no idea of consciousness, and either way, consciousness is functioning fine. This is why in some forms of spirituality there are no positive ways of stating what your true nature is. Other traditions describe it as "You are consciousness" or "You are awareness" or "You are the One." These are fine if we acknowledge that those positive descriptive words are relevant only through what they omit.

The self without form or shape or evaluation—that self that Merton calls "the unknown 'I'"—is unknown because it can never become an object of consciousness. Consciousness can never become an object unto itself; thoughts about consciousness are always within consciousness. This is the heart of the meditative mind, meditative observation, and Merton's contemplation: when we look inside for our true nature, we see that thoughts, images, and ideas are passing phenomena within our conscious experience. In doing so, we transcend those phenomena, because when all those notions and ideas and evaluations are gone, even for a few seconds, whatever we are is still there.

One of the challenges that people face when they begin to look for their true nature is this unconscious expectation that they are going to find themselves in the same way that they would find any other object. The Buddha recognized this when he came up with his doctrine of no self. He had a similar observation and a similar experience to Merton's: that the "I" we normally think we are is not a real I. Buddha went so far as to say there is no I and there is no self. What he saw was the false self—a bunch of conditioned patterns of thinking and feeling and reacting, none of which have any permanence. As fast as one self-referencing thought dies out, another one comes up and takes its place. When the Buddha realized this, he understood that everything we label "self" is not real. There is no self behind self-oriented thoughts that refer to a self that is not there when we look for it.

To say, "There is no self" is a negative way of putting it. I do not mean negative in the sense of bad; I mean negative in the sense of negating. Merton gave the view a positive spin when he called true nature "the unknown 'I'": the known "I" is an illusion, the unknown "I" is the I that cannot be made into an object. Whether we call that an "I," as he did, or "no self," as the Buddha did, is not important. We do not want to get too caught up in the terms that are being used, because that will distract us from opening to what these terms teach us.

This unknown self, or true nature, is always there—your true nature cannot go anywhere. When we realize this, we are realizing what was there all along. Realization in this sense is not about improvement; it is about recognizing what you always and already have been and always and already will be. It is not a discovery of a better self; rather, it is seeing that true nature transcends notions like consciousness and awareness, because "consciousness" and "awareness," like every word we use, are relevant only in terms of what they are not. "High" makes sense only in relation to "low," and "hot" makes sense only in relation to "cold." What defines consciousness is not consciousness.

Every word we use is understood not only by knowing what that word means, but by knowing what it is not. When I use a word like "sock," I am not referring to a car or an airplane or a cup—I am referring to a sock. You do not think of all the things that a sock is not when you use the term, because that would be inefficient, but as you learn the word, you learn that a sock is one thing, which means it is not all the others. When we come to true nature, it is not one thing as opposed to others: it is that all-inclusive expanse of being that transcends all the content of consciousness. It is the content within your mind—your thoughts, your feelings, all the rest—but also what you see when you open your eyes, what you feel, and what you hear. All of that is the content of your consciousness as well. But our true nature is that which has no opposite, has no "other" to it, and is not defined by what it is not.

You can see the challenge that we come up against: any languaging we use is going to be deceptive. How do we put into words the reality of you being beyond all ideas of you, all notions of self, and all constructions of self? Defining what true nature is will always put a limitation on it, and true nature does not include limitation. Words must be used and understood with a certain poetic sensibility, so that we are not stuck within the definitions—of God, Buddha nature, Brahman, or whatever you choose—for that which has no opposite, for your true nature.

Merton had a gift for expressing deep spiritual experience and insight through poetic language. I want to repeat his words: "Contemplation is precisely the awareness that this 'I' is really 'not I' and the awakening of the unknown 'I' that is beyond observation and reflection and is incapable of commenting upon itself." Sit with this and see how it lives in you over time. It is a beautiful way to open to the true self and to the unknown I that can never be made into an object of observation.

Always Already
Meditating

AWARENESS AND QUIET ARE THE MOST INTIMATE AND
OBVIOUS CHARACTERISTICS OF CONSCIOUSNESS.

Meditating is the core practice of most esoteric or inner forms of spirituality. Meditation in the way I use it is for waking up—"waking up" meaning the revelation of our true nature of what we are. But meditation can serve many different functions: it can relax you, it is good for your health, and it is especially good for your brain. You would think that we would give more attention to our mental, psychological, emotional, and spiritual hygiene. We have a hygiene for everything else—we brush our teeth, we keep our bodies clean, we keep our clothes clean, we straighten up our houses, and we take care of our cars. We give more attention to many of the inanimate objects in our life than we do to the well-being of our spirit, which makes us feel inspired and buoyant and gives us a direct sense and feel of the sacred and the timeless.

Whether one is spiritual or religious or not, we are all drawn to the sacred—a connection with a mysterious quality that lurks below the surface of our normal conscious attention. It is not that we need to go search for the sacred in the sense that it is hiding somewhere. The sacred is not hidden; it is the ground in which our whole life takes place, this ground of great significance, this feeling of meaning—not necessarily the definition of what that meaning might be, but the feeling of it—and the feeling of something profound and mysterious. This is what meditation, the art of deep inner listening, makes available to us.

When I teach meditation, I stress not only what we are doing but also the assumptions we bring to the simple practice of listening. We can view meditation as a form of spiritual seeking, of looking for something that we think we lack, or of trying to complete ourselves somehow, but meditation begins with the acknowledgment of what is already present, instead of the search for what is not or what we imagine is not present. One of the things I advise people to do when they sit down to meditate is to ask themselves a question: *Is it true that the peace, stillness, and quiet I am about to look for are not already present here and now?*

In those few seconds after you ask the question, if you are in a state of listening and of letting something other than a thought answer, your body and your consciousness can sense that there is a preexisting state of quiet and peace and that awareness itself is already present. Your mind may not be able to understand awareness, as it may not be able to grasp it, define it, see it, or touch it, but the mere fact that you can (for instance) hear someone's voice is possible only because of the preexisting state of awareness that is functioning right now. Just asking the question draws attention to this preexisting state of quiet, peace, and ease; it drives our attention spontaneously and intuitively to the awareness that is in the background of every experience.

That is why I call meditation "the art of listening"—listening, not with your mind or your ears, but with your entire being. Our whole bodies—physical body and subtle body—are extraordinarily sensitive living organisms, and these are what we use in meditation. I see meditation not only as the art of deep listening but also as the art of acknowledging what is always and already present. If we do not in some way acknowledge what is present, then we will try to seek or produce what we *imagine* not to be present. We must stop looking for something and chasing after something, even if that something is silence, stillness of mind, and peace. We must stop looking for these things as if they are absent from our current experience; they are the foundation of our current experience.

This form of meditation can be a radical shift from the way a lot of people meditate. It was for me. It took me by surprise when I finally noticed that much of what I was looking for in my meditation was already present before I began to meditate. I cannot quite convey the feeling when I sat down one day to meditate and observed that even before I was trying to be aware, awareness was already present, and that before I tried to settle in and be peaceful and still, there was already a state of peace and a sense of stillness. I realized that a lot of the qualities I was seeking in meditation were already present, and it was a shock. It was as if I had been poor my whole life and one day I put my hands in my pockets to find that they were full of money. I was a millionaire! I had assumed that I was poor and therefore never checked my pockets. I was trying to acquire money from the outside, but little did I know I already had it.

This is part of the meditation that I teach: acknowledgment of what is present instead of seeking what we imagine not to be present. That is a big difference from the way most folks meditate. It also addresses one of the reasons that so many people find meditation frustrating: their minds seem to be so busy, and they have difficulty settling down and listening. However, if we start with acknowledging that yes, awareness is already present, there is a sense of quiet or peace before we even look for it. It is as if these qualities are already the background of our conscious experience, but we are so caught up in *doing* that we never notice. Part of the doing we can be caught up in is active meditation itself, so that meditation becomes another form of looking for something and of trying to satisfy the relentlessly unfulfilled ego mind.

Awareness is present even if your mind is chatting away. In the same way that my voice produces sound, the thoughts in your mind produce an inner sound, but they happen within the quiet of awareness. Take a moment to feel that, to sense into it, and to listen to that background quiet. This awareness of quiet may be fleeting before your attention wanders, and that is okay; even when your attention wanders, there is still awareness that thought is happening within awareness and within consciousness—because if it was not, you would not even know that there was a thought.

Meditation is not the art of not thinking—that is a mistake about meditation that is made most of the time. It is the art of listening to that which already is not thinking, which is the space in which thoughts occur and the silence in which the noise of the mind chats to itself. So instead of trying to control your mind, to make it quiet or to make it think one thought, meditation makes thought irrelevant. It is another noise, and even when that noise of the mind is happening, it is happening within a quiet awareness or consciousness.

Awareness and quiet are the most intimate and obvious characteristics of consciousness. We are well served by acknowledging and noticing what is present rather than constantly searching for what is not. What is always and already present *is* always and already present, which means it is not apart from you, it is not other than you, and it is not something that is not now and always and already happening. When we are looking for something we imagine not to be here, that we imagine to be missing, the mind is talking to itself about what it thinks it needs to do. A mind that says, "I must quiet my mind" is still a noisy mind, and a mind that says, "I am not good at this" is a noisy mind. Notice how awareness is not battling with your mind. It is only the mind that battles with the mind, and it is only the mind that battles with how you feel, but even that battle is something that occurs within awareness.

It is more useful and certainly easier to think of meditation as the art of acknowledging what is already present. This can happen when you are sitting in meditation, which is great, but you can also do it at *any* time. It takes only a few seconds to notice that awareness and quiet are always and already the background of every experience. Start with little moments of meditation—ten seconds, fifteen seconds—and repeat them during the day. Gradually do nothing but this acknowledgment practice for two, ten, twenty, twenty-five seconds—whatever—but do not turn it into a battle, and do not turn it into something that is frustrating or makes you feel defeated. These small moments of meditation can change what you are noticing. In a certain sense, you will be changing your consciousness, opening and beginning to observe and feel and sense into—become sensitive to—the sacred and the timeless. It may or may not start out that way the first time you do it, but the sacred and the timeless are always and already present. All we need to do is take a moment to notice, and that is what meditation is.

When the Universe Contemplates Itself

THERE IS NO NOTHING.

Most of us have had the experience of looking up into the night sky. It is a process that captures the imagination as we gaze at the extraordinary expanse of space and contemplate the unbelievable mystery of how all this was created, how it works, and where it is going. There are so many questions that are unanswered. It is part of the beauty even in scientific investigation: when we find one truth, it brings to light ten other things that we did not know we did not know. Knowledge has that effect. It is wonderful and exciting and sometimes empowering to come to understand certain things about the nature of the cosmos.

When we are paying attention, we have a natural sense of awe. We are all here on this tiny planet floating in an immense and expanding sea of time and space. We are barely a pinprick, yet we are conscious beings. As far as we can look in this space, we can see a lot of things, but we have not encountered another intelligence with abilities that are like or beyond those of humans, at least not yet.

Of all the places we could be, of all the beings we could be, it is remarkable that in a certain sense we are the eyes and ears and the contemplating ability of the universe. Consciousness gives us this unique facility, not only to be aware, but also *to be aware that we are aware*. We can reflect on reflecting on things, and so what is happening is that the cosmos is reflecting upon itself. When we look at incredible mystery, spiritual awakening, or revelation itself, it will show that we—in the deepest sense of things—are the mystery that we are looking at.

The spiritual impulse—the impulse that motivates, drives, and inspires us to awaken to the deeper nature of reality—has a human element. In other words, as human beings we want whatever we want from that realization, whether that's happiness or love or a relief from suffering. But the real drive of awakening lies within life itself. This agenda is bigger than the human one: it is life or existence seeking to be conscious of itself and to know itself. If my talking about this ability of consciousness to recognize itself sounds a little too cosmic, you have my sympathies, but if you are quiet for a moment you will find that there is the simple sense of being—the sense of "I exist" even before you form the words "I exist." Even before thought defines that sense of being, there is a sense of existing and a sense of knowing that you exist. That is consciousness and what consciousness makes us capable of.

Imagine if we did not have consciousness, if we were robots, mechanically playing out a series of causes and effects on a biological, psychological, and emotional level, yet we had no sense of existing. It is impossible to conceive of the absence of consciousness, because in order to do so you must have consciousness to do the conceiving. That we can say anything about our subjective experience of life is itself proof of consciousness.

This is one of the wonderful aspects of the contemplative dimension of our life, where we spend some time looking within or being quiet. It connects us to these experiences of the mystery of existence, and not only to the mystery of galaxies and stars and other things that seem to be far off but also to the mystery of everyday things. We lose touch with the mystery of life, that sense of awe that brings us a feeling of vitality and engagement, because it is easy to get caught up in the details. There seem to be so many details and gadgets to keep track of the details that it is easy to be busy all the time, even when we do not need to be busy.

It has struck me for some years now that there is little difference between adults and babies in one regard: If you want to occupy a baby's attention, you put something bright and sparkly and colorful above their crib, and they will gaze at it and be swept up into the entertainment of what they are looking at. We adults do that with our cell phones. Our bright, shiny little things have practical uses, which sneakily makes our toys a necessity in daily living, at least for most people. As a result, it is easy to be distracted throughout the day, dealing with texts or emails or whatever must be done. The pace of contemporary life costs us the contemplative dimension, because it takes away the space to sit down, look up into the night sky, and ponder the mystery that we are and the mystery that we are taking part in.

My wife, Mukti, and I have quite a few oak trees—most of which are well over a hundred years old—on our property. Every autumn the oaks drop the acorns they produce, which is always wonderful because the acorns bring deer. We look out the window, see deer foraging, and marvel at the fact that those tiny acorns are the seeds for such expansive oak trees. A little thing, a seed, is the beginning of one of these amazing and majestic trees. It captures my imagination and my amazement that life can make anything and that there is anything rather than nothing. It seems like everything would be so much easier if there were nothing—it would take no effort, no explosions, no black holes, no supernovas. Yet there is no nothing; there is quite a bit of something.

That said, there still appears to be a lot more nothing than there is something in this universe. Nowadays scientists are scratching their heads and wondering what all this nothing is. When they look at it, they realize, "Wow, this nothing is not nothing! This nothing is something." "Nothing" is exerting the gravitational force. "Nothing" turns out not to be nothing. Scientists do not even know what this nothing is. They call it "dark matter," which is a spooky way of saying that the nothing that is there is something, but we do not know what it is. It is a mystery to us.

If someone were to ask you, "What is it like living in the world that you live in?" you might start to think of the world that human beings have created. Our creations are both impressive and a disaster at the same time. But compared to the mystery of existence? The simplest thing is extraordinarily mysterious if we pay much attention at all.

And not just things, but also people—our lovers, friends, children. If we care to look, if we contemplate anyone with any depth, it won't be long before we run into how mysterious they are.

Mukti and I have been married for more than two decades, and in one sense, as the years have gone on, we have gotten to know each other better and better, which is a lovely part of sharing your life with somebody. However, what I have noticed is that as we have gotten to know each other better, simultaneously the mystery of the other has shown up more. I find this a fascinating part of any human relationship: if we are paying attention—which is a big "if"—we see what an amazing mystery each person is. Even with people whom we think we know so well that we can predict their behavior or what they are going to be interested in or not interested in—even then, if we can look underneath the surface, life is full of mystery. When we lose touch with that, we become deadened. We become unconscious when we lose this connection with the absolute mystery of existence. Spirituality is an exploration of this mystery.

There is a difference, however, between the knowledge we acquire in the scientific disciplines and the knowledge we get through contemplation. The knowledge we get through the sciences is what we call objective knowledge, and the knowledge that we seek in spirituality is subjective knowledge. The neurons and electrons and synapses in your brain, the way your body chemistry works and your biology—that is objective knowledge. But you cannot treat yourself like a science project. That is why there is so much emphasis in spirituality on being aware and being present and seeing into your nature; you are seeing into the nature of your subjectivity, you are seeing the nature of consciousness itself, and that is a different exploration. Spirituality is a way of directly entering the subjective experience of being.

This is the nut that we crack in spirituality: opening the mystery of your own being through the act of contemplation, inquiry, and curiosity. Spirituality done well is the science of subjective experience. But again, even when we are doing that, we can get so tied up in the goal and what we hope to achieve—the state of being that we are trying to get to—that we will miss the *mysteriousness* of our being and the mysterious existence of consciousness. We are so busy trying to fix ourselves or achieve something that we do not slow down enough to notice the mysterious nature of our own existence, the mysterious nature of the sense of being and the sense of "I am." That we are even aware of being aware of existing is extraordinary. So far, we have not found that elsewhere in the universe; we may one day, but we do not know that.

The more we examine the nature of ourselves and the more we look for a self, the more we keep not finding. When we look inside to find our true self, our true nature, the first thing that happens is we do not find a self. We do not find this pseudoentity, even if it is only a psychological entity. Instead, we find a process—a process of moving thoughts and the feelings and emotions that those thoughts generate. If we look at each individual thought or behind each individual feeling, we will see that we cannot find a self in them. We can find the thought, but we cannot find the self that is having the thought; we can find a feeling, but what exactly is that "me" who is having the feeling?

One of the things that makes any spiritual discipline powerful is how seriously you take the inquiry, and by that I mean how precise you are. Sometimes in spirituality we let ourselves get away with a lot of imprecision. We are considering the nature of our being, and someone asks us, "Well, what do you find? What is the truth of your being?" We are hazy and muddled when it comes to how to express these things, and sometimes we are even hazy and muddled in terms of examining our experience or exploring our consciousness. Part of what gives any spiritual discipline its power is our ability to look in a precise way, not in a haphazard way.

What is the nature of my being? Where is this self? What is it exactly? Does it exist? If I am not a self, then what am I? These questions are not meant to have quick answers; they are meant to open your mind and open consciousness so that you can experience both mind and consciousness more directly and intimately. No matter where we look—from the biggest of the biggest to the smallest of the smallest—if we are paying attention, we cannot help but experience the awe and wonder of existence, and the awe and wonder of existence is what drives spiritual yearning. In a deeper sense, life's inherent inclination is to become fully conscious of itself: the feeling that you have of yearning or being driven spiritually is a desire that belongs to life itself wanting to be conscious of itself—to be fully awake and fully present. This is where the spiritual impulse is derived, from a place that is even deeper than our personal concern, deeper than what we hope for or what we want from our spirituality.

In other words, there is another game being played out on a completely different scale, and that is by life itself, by this immensity seeking to become as self-aware as it can. That is your connection to the mystery, and that is the origin of cosmic curiosity, whether it is curiosity about the vast scale of the cosmos that we find ourselves in or about the vast scale of the consciousness that we are. To engage with these things is so important; it is the reason why every form of deep spirituality emphasizes the ability to pay attention, to not walk through life on automatic pilot. One of the greatest potentials of spiritual practice, if we are doing it right, is that it takes us out of automatic pilot mode. It makes us conscious and aware of what is going on, of who we are, of what we are, and of how remarkable and unfathomable this world is and our being is. Consciousness itself is amazing—how it comes to life and how there is a consciousness of anything. That there is a consciousness of consciousness is mind-boggling.

Right down to the most ordinary events in life, everything is much more extraordinary than we give it credit for. To engage with the true nature of ourselves—with the mysterious and overwhelming quality of existence—requires us to pay attention, to be present, and to not sleepwalk through the next moment and the next day and the next week and the next year. It requires us to endeavor to bring even a deeper sense of consciousness and awareness to each moment. When we do, the quality of our consciousness itself transforms our whole being.

It is an incredible experience to go outside, look up at the sky, and contemplate the overwhelmingly vast distances that make up this universe that we find ourselves part of and that we discover ourselves to be the consciousness of. When we are contemplating the universe, we are the universe contemplating itself, and that may be the most wondrous and extraordinarily profound aspect of our whole life.

Conscious of
Consciousness

I MIGHT NOT BE WHAT I HAVE BEEN THINKING.

As I have been suggesting, a big part of our spiritual impulse origi-
nates from life itself. Each person has their own hopes and dreams,
but if we could push aside our expectations of what we might get
out of spirituality, at a much deeper, more fundamental level, what
is happening is life or existence is seeking to become conscious of
itself and fully aware of itself. This is the drive of spirituality, and in
another sense, it is also the drive of a lot of science. Science is the
way the universe explores itself objectively, as an object or as a series
of objects, and spirituality is how life contemplates itself subjectively.
To contemplate the nature of consciousness is to contemplate your
most subjective experience of being.

The word "subjective," at least in English, is not necessarily a com-
pliment. When you tell somebody they are being subjective, it means
they are caught in a particular viewpoint and they can't see outside of
it. That aspect of the word "subjectivity" carries a lot of baggage. Some
of that baggage is not positive, but the way I am using "subjective" is
neither positive nor negative; I am using it in a matter-of-fact way.
Spiritual disciplines are a way of exploring our subjective experience
of being. When you go inside, when you meditate, you are trying to
engage your most subjective sense of being.

There are direct and indirect ways of doing this, but I am more inclined toward the direct. The difficulty is that it is not complicated. It would be easier if it *were* complicated, because it would give our busy minds a lot more to do, but it is not. When I talk about examining the subjective nature of our being, I mean turning within to our subjective experience. Usually when we think of "my subjective experience of being," we are referring to what we think, what we feel, our opinions, or our beliefs. However, those things (the thinking, feeling, and experiencing) are not subjective in the end, at least not in the sense that I am using the word. They are not the most subjective experience of being, because our thoughts and feelings arise within conscious awareness, exist for a short time, and then they pass away. But we have an experience of awareness even if we are not thinking or feeling anything.

When we start to explore the nature of our consciousness, consciousness is already there. At this very moment, consciousness is right here. We do not need to do anything to create consciousness. In a certain sense, there is an understandable usefulness in trying to create consciousness, trying to create more awareness, and trying to be extra mindful—but a more direct way of being mindful is to acknowledge the presence of consciousness, of awareness, and the fact that it is already operating. It is operating right now, and it is why you can read these words. That is the reason you can feel whatever you feel about consciousness or think whatever you think about it and reflect upon that—consciousness makes that possible.

One of the mistakes people make when they seek a deeper understanding or a more direct experience of consciousness is to go looking for consciousness as if it were a thought thing or as if what they needed was a better definition of consciousness. They look for it as if it were an object, but consciousness is not an object; it is your most subjective experience in being. Just as your eyeball cannot see itself, consciousness cannot make itself into an object of perception, because it is always the ultimate subject.

When we are considering the nature of our consciousness, the first thing we do comes from a place of not trying to understand and not trying to figure all this out, because these are thoughts and we must go deeper than thought. Thought is not our most subjective experience of being, although many people would think that it is because their experience of themselves is a ceaseless, restless thinking about themselves. However, it turns out that when we look closely, we notice that all those thoughts are objects that appear to consciousness and to awareness.

The object and our experience are what I sometimes call "the content." To boil it down to something simple, there is the *content* of our experience, which we pick up through our senses—what we see, taste, touch, feel, think, and imagine, this is all the content of our consciousness—and then there is the *context* in which all experience, all thoughts, all feelings, all emotions, and all perception happen. The context is not itself a thought or a feeling, but it is the space and the awareness in which thought and feeling arise. If you get into spiritual practice and you are waiting for some big experience to happen—some experience that will be the culminating experience of all other experience—it keeps you obsessed with the content, and it keeps you obsessed with what does or can or might appear in your consciousness at some point in time. But whatever can appear in your consciousness now or at any other point in time will also pass. Everything that appears in or to your consciousness is, in a sense, in movement; it is not static, for nothing lasts long, and it is not eternal. That is the nature of the content.

The Buddha would have said that content is impermanent, yet we are continually grasping at the content. Sometimes someone who is more intellectually hooked up thinks they will be saved by having the right types of thinking, the right series of thoughts, or the right intellectual understanding, and so they are endlessly seeking a more subtle, clear conceptual understanding. Somebody that is more emotionally based will spend their time in spirituality—unless they are careful—looking to have the right experience or the right feeling. Their searching will happen on the level of feeling and emotion, but feeling and emotion are also things that arise within consciousness.

To explore the nature of consciousness is tricky because it is the ultimate simplicity. We are used to looking for objects of our experience or anticipating an experience, but when we are looking at the nature of consciousness, we see that consciousness is the common element of all experience. There is no such thing as having an experience that you are not conscious of or a perception that you are not conscious of, as there is always an element of consciousness. To explore the nature of consciousness is different from exploring the nature of thought—although I am using words here, which are symbols for thoughts, to try to direct consciousness to reflect upon itself. In the end, we are not looking for the "right" conceptual understanding, and we are not looking to have the "right" experience—though a lot of spiritual seekers get hung up on looking for the optimal understanding or experience.

Consciousness is the context in which all experiences and all understanding happen. Consciousness transcends understanding or thought, and it also transcends experience. This can be confusing for many folks, because we are conditioned to try to grasp at consciousness in terms of understanding or experience—that is, to grasp at the content—and in doing so, we miss the context. The context, again, of every experience and of every perception is consciousness itself—is awareness itself.

You need not understand consciousness or awareness at all. That is not necessary, as consciousness will function whether you understand it or not. We start out with an acknowledgment: *Whether I understand it or not, consciousness is present right now at this moment. Consciousness is present, and awareness is present.* If we add in the element of a contemplation, we add in an inquiry. When we are exploring the nature of consciousness, we are also exploring the nature of ourselves and of what we are. Part of this is about getting back to consciousness as such, instead of consciousness *of something*. What helps us to do that is to discriminate between the content and the context: the context is consciousness or awareness itself, and the content is everything else. When you can make this simple distinction between the two, then you can start to have a clear, deep knowing of consciousness, because you won't get stuck grasping at the content.

Trying to grasp at awareness is like trying to grasp at space. Consciousness or awareness is like that; I liken it to space because you cannot grasp it, as there is nothing there. It is a kind of light, but I do not mean a light you can see. It is the light that makes it possible to see. If you lost consciousness for more than a minute, there would be the slow, gradual dissolving of the awareness of anything. If consciousness or awareness were to disappear, there would be no experience of anything; there would not even be the experience of nothing, and there would not even be the experience of a void. If there is zero consciousness, zero awareness, then there is no experience of anything.

This consciousness makes our whole experience of being possible because consciousness *is* our whole experience of being in its true sense. As you read this, you are conscious, there is consciousness operating, and there is awareness operating. You do not have to try to do anything to be conscious; this is not a practice of trying to become more conscious or more aware, this is a process of acknowledging awareness and acknowledging consciousness. It is here. What we are doing is getting a sense of consciousness and a sense of how awareness feels, you might say, even though consciousness and awareness are beyond the feeling, because all feelings are just stuff that arises.

When we become more aware of awareness, more conscious of consciousness, we start to feel things intuitively; it is the body's way of recognizing consciousness. That is why I suggest spiritual practice boils down to trying to get the sense and the feel of consciousness, the sense and the feel of awareness, hanging out in those feelings, and then recognizing that every conceptual way of thinking about yourself and describing yourself is an object of consciousness. These things can disappear, yet you as consciousness remain. Every thought, every belief, and every opinion is in motion. They move through consciousness, and they move through awareness, which is why you think them over and over again, because all the concepts are disappearing as fast as they arise.

Imagine that the mind had stopped creating thoughts, reactions, feelings, and all of that stuff; imagine that it ceased for a moment. In that moment, you will have lost your familiar ways of defining yourself, yet even when all those familiar labels are gone, there is still this basic sense of awareness and a basic sense of consciousness. What you are can exist without all the ways of defining or judging yourself, because what you are transcends all those. In other words, you still exist even when you are not thinking thoughts about yourself.

You do not exist as your thoughts. If all the thoughts in your mind were to stop for five seconds, these would be five seconds when the egoic self did not exist, because the egoic self is the movement of thinking and the associated feelings and emotions your thinking produces. If you could *not* think about yourself, you would lose your entire sense of self. You *as you are* would not disappear, but you *as you imagine you are* would.

As you let go of everything you imagine you are—good, bad, indifferent—you might start to intuit the prior existing state of being, which is consciousness itself and awareness itself. This is part of contemplation: an exploration of the nature of consciousness and the nature of self. It is a meditative act—you might even sense this as you read these words—because getting down to the core nature of the self requires us to go beyond more objective aspects of awareness. You must get underneath all the ways you have defined yourself and realize that whatever you are exists without any definition whatsoever, yet it still exists and it still is. Begin to get the sense of, *My God, I might not be what I have been thinking I have been my whole life! I might have been mistaken, and everybody I know may have been mistaken as well. I might be something different from who I imagined myself to be.*

This is a space that starts to expand when we look closely. We sense a great possibility that we could be free of the person we imagined ourselves to be and are something entirely different. You can start to get a feel and a sense for the mystery of your being, your consciousness, and see for yourself that consciousness or awareness is the prior condition and the context in which all experience and all perception arises.

Contemplation is inherently a meditative act because it is the only way to pay attention. I do not mean you should be twisted up in the full lotus position; I mean that it is meditative in the sense of your being able to enter the quiet spaces of your being. The quiet spaces are not hard to find, as the quietness is all there, and it is the atmosphere in which everything is occurring. To contemplate ourselves, our being, and consciousness itself is not necessarily as hard as we imagine. It is more immediate and more direct than we might think. None of this is difficult because it is complicated; if it is difficult at all, it is because it is so immediate and because you cannot figure it out in your mind.

If you are trying to do it right and get it all right in your mind, you are still lost in the conceptual dimension. There is a time to use the conceptual dimension of your mind—it is a powerful and potentially creative and useful tool, no doubt about that—yet when we consider the deeper nature of our being, the constant movement of thought can be deceptive because it makes us feel like we *are* that thinking and we *are* our self-definition and the associated emotions and feelings that it generates.

This is not only about you. This is about anything or anybody. What we know about somebody is a bunch of information—a bunch of ideas, images, snapshots from the past, judgments in the present, and conclusions—all of which is in the mind and which may have some use sometimes, although not as much as we think. This is not about contemplating only you, for a deep contemplation of your nature is a doorway into all of nature and all of existence. It is not a self-centered or narcissistic act if we do it correctly, because it helps us wake up from our narcissistic self-obsession. The self that most human beings are obsessed with is the self that exists in their mind and only in their mind as they fight for it, protect it, assert it to others, or even try to be a better or enlightened person. As useful and powerful as thought is, it also has a quality to it that can almost send consciousness into a trance as soon as we think that all the truth of anything lies in the definition we give it.

"Nothing" is the word we give it, and "nothing" is exactly the way we have defined it. Contemplation is a means of peeling back the overlay and seeing what is underneath. This is not a difficult thing to do inherently. We need not go deep into our consciousness to do this—not at all. We merely need to be able to stay present right here and right now to the obviousness of consciousness. The challenge lies in staying with this one simple thing. It is much harder to stay with one simple thing with real consistency than to go into complexity. Complexity will entertain you endlessly and give your mind something to do, but coming into direct contact with consciousness itself is the ultimate simplicity because there is nothing to hold on to. You cannot grasp consciousness as awareness, nor can you lose it. You might get distracted and start obsessing about the next thought or the next feeling, but even then, all your obsessing is happening within consciousness, so we never, ever get away from consciousness.

For all the striving people do to get into consciousness or to find consciousness, the funny truth is that you cannot lose it. You can lose consciousness *of* consciousness—you can be conscious without ever having noticed that you are conscious, without ever reflecting upon it, or without recognizing what an extraordinary and mysterious thing it is. The reason we can miss it is because it is omnipresent and it is part of every experience. Consciousness itself does not stand out; it is all the other stuff that stands out. By contemplating the nature of consciousness within ourselves, we are setting the stage for consciousness to become illumined and for it to recognize itself directly, because consciousness can wake up from the identification with its content.

This does not mean there is anything wrong with the content. There is nothing wrong with thinking or feeling. Trying not to think does not work well, and trying not to feel is a way of living in denial. I am not encouraging you to toss away every thought you ever had or never to feel anything again, as it is the *identification* with thoughts and feelings that is problematic. Simply notice that in your deepest being, you do transcend it all, the self-seeking thoughts and self-referential emotions. You stand prior to them, and they can and do disappear while you as consciousness remain. Noticing this in a direct way sets the stage for the flash of recognition—that way in which, not the mind, but consciousness itself recognizes itself. It is as if consciousness says, "Aha! I have been lost in thought, and I have been lost in feeling, and I have been lost in the past, and I have been lost in my ideas of the future and all that I thought I was—and none of it defines who I am." What a revelation! What a great freedom to realize. This is the heart of contemplation.

We do not have to be in some twisted state of consciousness to reach this. Your garden-variety consciousness will do, and your garden-variety experience is perfectly adequate for seeing that the context of experience outlasts the content. Content comes and goes, but the context is always here. What does that say about you?

This is what I mean by contemplation: to look at something. This is what meditation is, this is what inquiry is, and this is how we come to know ourselves differently than we ever have. This is how we get to discern what we call "others" and the world in a way that we could never have imagined—a way that is not apart from us. Contemplating the subjective sense of consciousness, the subjective sense of self, makes us vulnerable to liberating insight. Think of how much time most people spend in their spiritual practice obsessed with modifying the content of their experience; year after year after year they are looking for the right experience and the right content. What a surprise when they finally wake up and realize it was the context that was the most important or liberating aspect of spiritual contemplation. This gives them a whole new basis for action, for relating, and for contributing to this world of ours. Waking up is not a self-centered act—in the end it is what frees us up from self-centeredness if we do it correctly. Hopefully it frees us up to have a joyful and benevolent presence in the world, which speaks to our deepest sense of being. If we can be a benevolent, conscious, and free presence in the world, we have something truly revolutionary to offer: to be.

Know Thyself

WHEN WE LOOK INSIDE,
WE SEE THAT WHATEVER WE ARE IS *PRIOR* TO THOUGHT.

It is said that the ancient Greeks engraved the phrase "Know thyself" at the entrance to the Temple of Apollo at Delphi. The implication is that knowing yourself was the currency that would allow you to enter the temple. We can see this in terms of a building with an inscription that is communicating the importance of self-knowledge as you walk in the door of the sacred space. But there is also a metaphorical meaning. If we see the temple as the repository of the truth of who we are—the truth of existence—then to enter that truth, we must know ourselves.

This is not any ordinary knowledge; it is not the acquisition of facts, memories, and stuff that happened throughout our lives. This is not the knowledge read in a book or gained from studying psychology or theology. This is something more immediate and more intimate. To realize what we are, we must spend time with ourselves. It is a funny thing to say, because we all think we are spending time with ourselves all the time and that, in fact, we cannot get away from ourselves. But I am talking about spending time with yourself in a deep way—that is, to enter contemplation, a quiet but intent observation of the unfolding of experience and consciousness. Contemplating consciousness is an investigation and requires a quiet looking and seeing. It is driven by the intention to come to a deep experiential knowing of what you are.

Two paths appear when we start to contemplate the nature of our being. The first is what I call "enlightened relativity": "enlightened" because it is seeing the truth of ourselves in a direct and immediate way; "relativity" because it is a relative way of exploring that truth—it is not absolute.

Think of a tree. We assume it is made up of roots, trunk, branches, and leaves—that is how we define the word "tree." It is a ridiculous definition! Have you ever experienced a tree that is alive, healthy, and vibrant? Have you ever seen a healthy tree that was separate from the soil? Have you ever seen a tree that has thrived without sun? Can you imagine a tree in an environment without air and rainfall? If there is no such thing as a growing, living tree that is ever apart from the soil, from the sky, from the sun, or from the rain, this tells us something that runs contrary to our conditioned viewpoint: a tree does not exist apart from its environment. Since we never, ever find a tree isolated from its environment, we must conclude that a tree *is* its environment. This is a rational way of giving a label (like "tree") to the experience of a type of unity. It takes an entire cosmos to create a tree, and that cosmos is expressing itself in the form of a single tree. When we see this truth beyond even the most rational understanding, we take that next leap and perceive that everything is all-inclusive. In other words, a single tree is also the entire cosmos, and the entire cosmos is a single tree.

Apply this thinking to human beings. On a relative level, we too exist as the whole environment. Although we may think that we are separate from the world, it takes an entire cosmos to produce you and me and the billions of other people on the planet. You can test and see how separate you are right now: hold your breath for twenty seconds, and you will start to become uncomfortable, because you are cutting your body off not only from something that it needs but from something that *it is*. Take oxygen away from a human being, and you no longer have a human being.

When we break down what the environment is, we find it is made of the same stuff that we are. As the wonderful spiritual writer Alan Watts said in his lecture "The Nature of Consciousness," "Look, here is a tree in the garden and every summer it produces apples, and we call it an apple tree because the tree 'apples.' That's what it does. Alright, now here is a solar system inside a galaxy, and one of the peculiarities of this solar system is that, at least on the planet Earth, the thing peoples! In just the same way that an apple tree apples!" Think about that: the world *peoples* in the same way that an apple tree *apples*. Just as an apple tree produces apples, because apples are part of the apple tree, earth produces human beings. No earth, no human beings.

This is one way to look at the aphorism "Know thyself." We start from a conventional standpoint, examine the conventions we have, and see that the reason we exist in an environment is because we were always *of* that environment. This is knowledge in a transcendental sense; it is not rational knowledge, nor is it irrational, but it is transrational. Transrational knowledge shows us that there is no separation between any humans, right down to the blood and bones and marrow and the entire environment. As the great spiritual teacher Nisargadatta Maharaj memorably said, "When I look within and see that I am nothing, that is wisdom. When I look without and see that I am everything, that is love. Between these two, my life turns."

If we invert this statement, we find the second path to contemplating the nature of our being. We look inside and search for our true self, our true nature, and what we truly are. We are considering the content of consciousness. As we do so we realize that *everything* is the content of consciousness, even the external world, because without consciousness, we cannot perceive the world. When we turn the tide of investigation inward, we will notice all the things we are *not*. We will see that we won't find ourselves in our definition of ourselves. If we examine all the thoughts we use to define ourselves, we will realize there is no self within those thoughts. Thoughts come and go, but the perception of thought stays. You cannot *be* a thought or a collection of thoughts, no matter how sophisticated those thoughts are.

When we look inside, we see that whatever we are is *prior* to thought. You were there before thought, you were there during the thought, and you are going to be there after thought. I am not talking about the you that thought creates—that disappears as soon as you stop thinking about it. If you accept that our true nature does not exist in our thinking minds, then where should you look for it to know thyself?

Start with what you feel. When you investigate what you feel, the sensation is one of being right here, right now. How does the ground under your foot feel? How does your body feel? How does your mind feel? What is the feel of the space you are in? Get a sense of these things. The feelings come and go too, as they are always changing, so you cannot *be* what you feel. You will have feelings and sensations and emotions—those are perfectly fine things—but they do not tell you about what you are. I always think of this contemplation as being like doing a science experiment. You have got to look at it in that way, and you cannot let yourself off the hook with fuzzy thinking. You might say to yourself, "The question before us is: 'Am I my thoughts or not?' The only way to find that out is to ask: 'When I stop thinking, do I disappear?'" The thought-based self disappears, but something is still there: your consciousness. It is the consciousness that is thinking about my words right now, that is feeling what you feel, and that is seeing what you see.

The strange thing is when we look inside for ourselves, the more we look, the less we find. So we keep looking . . . and looking. Eventually, as we keep *not* finding the self, it will dawn on us, *I am not finding myself in the content of my experience, because the content is constantly changing, yet whatever it is that I am seems always to be here. The content of my consciousness is not telling me who I am.*

Let's go back to the teaching of Nisargadatta Maharaj, which is hard to beat: "When I look within and see that I am nothing, that is wisdom. When I look without and see that I am everything, that is love. Between these two, my life turns." He did not say, "When I look within and see nothing" or "see that I am looking at nothing," because these are projections of the mind. Instead he said, "[I] see that I *am* nothing." That is a revelation: to look inside and to see that it is not that there is nothing, it is that we *are* that nothing. When you have found that "nothing," an incredible sense of relief, freedom, happiness, and well-being arises—symptoms of coming back to our senses, or, as we say in spirituality, waking up.

To "know thyself" by looking inside is to see beyond thoughts, sensations, memories, imagination, and self-centered thinking, because none of that is you. It is strange, because you keep not finding anything until you bump into the finding that "I *am* that nothing" and awaken to that reality. It's the fullest nothing you are ever going to bump into! It is not like an empty box of nothing, it is not the nothing you find in the dictionary, but it is a being of nothing. Consciousness is nothing; your awareness of these words is nothing, too.

Consider this in terms of love. When you experience love, ask yourself, *How much does it weigh? What color is it? What does it sound like?* You realize that love is not a something, it is a nothing—but that does not mean that love does not exist or that you do not experience it. Love is not a thing, and it is not even an experience. It can be experienced as experience, but anybody who has kids knows that you do not always feel a huge gushing in your heart chakra for your child. You might much of the time, but if your toddler is throwing a fit in the grocery store or your teenager is screaming at you, you are not thinking, *Oh my God, I am so in love with my child right now.* Does that mean that you do not love your child? Of course not. Real love is there even when you do not feel a lot of love; real love transcends the momentary experience of love. Imitation love, on the other hand, disappears as soon as your feeling state disappears; it is an adolescent love at best.

When we look inward, we discover we are nothing and realize that nothingness is full, it is profound, and it is what we are. When we look outward, we see that everything is connected to everything else. Whether you choose to look outward or inward, you will find your true nature. Paradoxically, we are everything and nothing—everything *is* nothing, and nothing *is* everything. This makes no sense if we stay in abstract ideas, but it makes absolutely perfect sense in direct experience, if we can get to direct experience.

Know thyself. Looking inside and seeing that we are nothing; looking outside and seeing that we are everything: these are the entry points into the divine.

You Are the Total Environment

EVERYTHING IS ITS ENVIRONMENT,
AND THE ENVIRONMENT IS EVERY INDIVIDUAL THING.

Spiritual teachings are meant to get us to a half-realized place and eventually to take us beyond that state to awakening. Often this requires learning to use the power of our discrimination, not in a philosophical or purely intellectual way, but to connect that intellectual process to our direct experience. There are many teachings that will say things like, "Notice that while thoughts are present, you are not your thoughts. Thoughts come and go. Whatever you are, you are that which watches the thoughts come and go, so thoughts are at best a secondary reality. You are not your feelings, because your feelings are also something that are occurring to you—whatever you are—and they are also coming and going, and there is at least a feeling that you remain as a constant."

This is a common spiritual strategy or technique. I think of it as meditative discrimination—"meditative" meaning it is intended to connect us with our actual experience in the moment, and it is not dogma or philosophy. What we are doing is pushing consciousness into the witness state, because in the spiritual exercise of using discrimination, we are learning to disidentify (which is different than disassociate) from defining ourselves by our thoughts or feelings or

112 THE MOST IMPORTANT THING

even the world around us. We realize that we are awareness, as opposed to, well, everything else, or anything we are aware of.

When we perceive ourselves as consciousness, as awareness itself, it is life changing. This a significant insight, and we can even call it its own kind of awakening—a fundamental shift out of identification with thoughts and feelings to the purely subjective experience of being consciousness or awareness—*but it is not an end point.* It is a midpoint of realization. We still have a fundamental difference between the perceiver and the perceived, between awareness or consciousness and everything that awareness or consciousness is aware of or conscious of. Next come the deeper states of realization, when the perceiver or the witness state collapses and when the perception of subject and object collapses. That is when we find our truth about the nature of our existence.

What does it mean when the subject and object collapse? What is the experience of that like? The best way to describe this is that you realize you are the total environment. You *are* wherever you might find yourself at any time. Again, think about a tree. When you start to look at it, you will see that the way we have been taught to think about what a tree *is* is as an abstraction. For the sake of convenience and communication, we sacrifice something by reducing things in the natural world down so that we can communicate about them, and we think we know them and have power over them. The price we pay for that is we forget that a tree does not exist without soil, sky, rain, clouds, and space—without its environment.

We are so abstract in our thinking that we argue, "No, a tree depends on the sun, it depends on the soil, and it depends on the rain for its survival," but it does not *depend* on these things; they exist together as one thing. To realize this unity is to realize that everything exists as a coherent whole: "I am the whole thing; in no way am I separate or other than the whole thing." Your body, the thoughts in your head, your feelings, the blood coursing through your veins, your heartbeat, your breath—everything that makes you what we call "human" depends upon the whole environment. There would be no human beings without sunshine, because it would be like existing billions of miles out in cold space, yet most of us do not readily think, "I am the sunshine," unless we are a realized being or a saint.

Everything is its environment, and the environment is every individual thing. As William Blake wrote:

To see a World in a Grain of Sand
And a Heaven in a Wild Flower
Hold Infinity in the palm of your hand
And Eternity in an hour . . .

That is what the experience of unity is kind of like. I say "kind of" because no description is the same as what it describes, but perhaps if you hold this description in a light way, in an easy way, and contemplate it, you will wake up one day and realize there are different ways of seeing and experiencing life. We have been taught to experience the world and ourselves as bits that we can name and classify and discriminate one from the other, but in the end, these bits do not have their own independent existing reality. They never would have arisen without their environment, nor could they even exist without it.

Experience Prior
to Thought

ALL OF EXISTENCE IS GOD,
INCLUDING THE ONE THAT RECOGNIZES THAT.

Have you ever noticed that when you explore the truth of one thing, you run into the truth of everything? In the conceptual mind this seems like a mystical insight, and sometimes it is—truth can come to us as a revelation. But it is also true, at least to a lesser degree, if we bring our intelligence and conceptual mind to bear upon how interconnectedness is a living fact. This is not a clever idea, it is not a spiritual idea, and it is not even a spiritual thing, but it is the way existence is. Just as there is no such thing as a tree without its environment, there is no human being without the rest of existence. Our abstract definition of what a body is does not include the earth, the sky, the wind, the rain, and the oxygen, but if we deprive ourselves of any of those things, we will not exist. Take the sun away, and you will not exist. Take oxygen away, even for only a few minutes, and we will be gone, not only because we need oxygen, but also because we *are* oxygen.

I know that for some people this is difficult to understand even on a conceptual level, because we are taught to think of each thing as separate from all the other things. But without all the elements of this earth, there is no human being. The earth manifests itself as a human being, and the human being is the earth. Furthermore, there is no earth without the galaxy. I recently learned that scientists have discovered we have about ten times more galaxies in the cosmos than previously thought; they now estimate there to be a trillion galaxies. *A trillion.* To cross the Milky Way would take untold light-years, and there are a trillion of these things. It is overwhelming how massive, how expansive, and how wondrous the cosmos is. That is awe-inspiring when you let it sink in.

It takes all those universes to create one you, because without them, you would not be. Without this cosmos, there would be no human being. Our thought breaks the world into pieces, and that is fine. That is not a criticism of thought, because that is all thought can do: it must break the world into pieces, and then it can reassemble those pieces like a computer does. Although remember that computers did not exist until there was a mind that could conceptually tear the world apart, configure it in different and unique ways, and create a new piece of technology called a computer with which to reassemble the pieces.

We do this with language, with concepts, and with ideas.

The ability to conceptualize, have ideas, and see how they impose a separation upon existence that is not inherent to existence has a utilitarian purpose, but that does not mean that the way concepts break the world into pieces and describe the pieces as independently existing is true about existence itself. Everything is interconnected, even if we tend to think of the world as a bunch of separate things.

We are not only interconnected, though interconnectedness is the best way to describe the experience of seeing how our concept of things, our idea of things, and our definition of things interconnect with one another. Going even deeper than that, we can say that things do not interconnect with one another—they *are* one another. That is the deeper understanding, yet it is still a surface comprehension of unity. This truth is in plain sight; we do not need extraordinary intelligence to see it. We live so much in the world of concepts that we forget that they are dividing something apart that is indivisible, that our concepts are in disagreement with the actual direct perception of things, and that we have come so far into the conceptual realm that we stop experiencing and perceiving things directly. This is a big part of what enlightenment is: the ability to perceive directly, without looking through a lens of concepts or ideas. Awakening is when we finally experience our being without the interface of any conceptual understanding. What we wake up from is the conceptual world.

Do not worry. Once you wake up from this, it is not like you lose language or you cannot use concepts anymore. Instead, you may begin to live and perceive from a different state of being and a different state of consciousness than one that is defined through conceptual understanding. This is what spiritual inquiry is for—we use ideas and questions like "What am I?" or "Who am I?" and start to see that if we take any single concept or group of concepts, we do not find any self in them. We might instead realize that the truth of our being is not defined by any concept, and if we do see that, we will have an awakening, which feels like we woke up from a dream. That is because we did! We woke up from the living dream of perceiving everything through the conceptual mind.

This conceptual mind is a storyteller. Our description of anything is a narrative; it is not exactly the way things are in direct perception or direct experience. It is good to explore the nature of ideas and concepts, the structure of language, and what effect language has upon our minds and upon the way we perceive and experience life. Until we can see that, we are perceiving and experiencing life through the whole host of concepts and ideas that we have, and there is little hope of waking up and of perceiving the reality of you or anybody or anything else beyond concepts or ideas. But waking up does not mean you do not have ideas, and it does not mean you cannot employ them for creative and practical purposes; it means that your sense of reality is no longer held hostage to them. This is how spiritual teachings guide us into the unknown.

Many different esoteric teachings and religions talk about the great unknown, and as seekers we often try to think of it as being like a place, perhaps an interior place, called "The Unknown," because we think we are referring to nothing more than an idea. That is an incomplete understanding: the unknown is a way of describing the direct experience of each instant instead of through the indirect, distorting mechanism of thought. When we are not experiencing and perceiving each moment through the distorting lens of thought, we are having a direct experience of what is. Then *and only then* do we experience absolute unity and absolute oneness—the whole world is one's own being and all of existence is God, including the one who recognizes that.

The most rational and powerful place to start is with yourself. Perceive the moment and yourself outside of any concept, outside of any idea, outside of story, outside of memory, and outside of narrative. When you do, all the distortions can stop, and with them "you"—the "you" who has been defined in memory and concepts and ideas—stop too. For some people, this is frightening to contemplate, because their "self" is the only self they have ever known, and they believe it is the only self there ever is. If it is all imagined, then when we stop imagining it, it is not there. However, whatever we are is still here, but no longer defined or experienced through mind, concepts, and ideas.

The challenge of any inner form of spiritual work is not perceiving through the mind, concepts, ideas, memory, beliefs, or opinion. All that takes thought, and we exist whether there is thought or not. Remember, the reality of anything is not the idea we have of anything—including yourself, including the world, including others, and including God. The idea that you have of any of those things is not what they are; it is an idea. What are any of those, what are you, your neighbor, your friend, what is the world, what is existence, without reference to a single thought? If you keep looking for a complementary thought, you will be confused, but if you let it go, you will come into (at least for a moment) a place where it is all unknown. You will not know who you are anymore, and you will not know who your friend is or your neighbor is. You will not know what the world is, because you are not looking for the mind to give you a conceptual representation of any of those things. You have arrived at something more than a representation—at something real.

The real is not to be found in a representation, but it is to be found *directly*—immediately before thought. Then we can employ thought all we want, because thought can be what it is: a tool. Every one of the words on this page stands for something that is not the word, and it is the same with thoughts. Some thoughts represent things—a thought tree represents a tree, and a thought person represents a human being—but a human being is not the thought person any more than a tree is the thought tree. When we start to suspend the mind, we see that thought may be useful—even creative at times—but it is not going to show us what anything truly is. Then we have the potential to directly perceive existence and our being. That is where awakening can occur.

Even when we have awakened, we must be careful not to start believing the thoughts we have about our awakening. Here it gets tricky. Some people awaken and start thinking, *Well, I am awakened; therefore what I think is true.* That is a truly ridiculous statement. Some thoughts may be more exact representations of reality than others, and all thoughts are not equally untrue. Some are closer to the truth, some are further away, some have nothing to do with it, and some do not even represent anything except other thoughts. So, lest we continue to live until our last breath in what amounts to a conceptual, abstract world—a world that is representative rather than real—we must break out of that. When we do, it feels extraordinary, like, *Aha! I may have a history, I may have those thoughts, I may have representations, and I may have images of the past and the present moment, but those are not what I am. They do not define me. They can never be big enough to capture the reality of anything.* It is said the thought water is not going to quench your thirst, no matter how sophisticated your understanding of that thought is.

The thought is not the thing that it represents. Try to get that right down to your core, right down to the marrow in your bones and into the blood that flows through your veins: *the thought is not the thing.* Then embrace that intermediary step of unknowing things, and as you enter the unknown, you'll see it is not a place; it is the living reality of things underneath the idea of the unknown. The point is not to spend the rest of your life saying, "I do not know" to everything; it is to step out of the known and directly perceive. You do this by entering the lived reality of not knowing, which takes you out of the known, out of the idea and to the reality of you, of anything, and of anyone. It's a place where words are useful tools, but you are no longer trapped by them.

The Simple Joy
of Being

IT IS USEFUL TO REFLECT ON WHAT HAPPINESS IS.

The Sierra Nevada mountain range near Lake Tahoe is one of the most beautiful spots in the world. Some of my best memories of my youth are of times spent there. Some of the mountains are high for North America—14,000-foot peaks—and it is difficult, rugged terrain, but powerful and gorgeous. In my twenties, I would go up to the John Muir Trail and backpack for weeks, even months, absorbed in silence and the absolute majesty of the environment. The mountains were my religious temple; I called them my cathedral. They were a place of great inspiration, peace, and stillness. I have always felt connected to those mountains.

A couple of years ago I was driving up there by myself to do a retreat. It takes about four hours to get to the Sierras from where I live. As soon as I reached the foothills, I laughed loudly and deeply for a good ten minutes with the joyousness of being back in those mountains. I have been to other places that are beautiful and profound, wildernesses that I enjoy immensely, but nothing is like the Sierras for me.

Part of the beauty of being in the mountains, especially when you are backpacking, is that it is a serious place to be, especially if you are up there alone and weeks away from any road. You must take care of yourself. You cannot be casual about it, as you cannot afford to break an ankle—it could be a long time before someone comes by. Even though these wild spaces are beautiful and sacred and brimming with a feeling of the divine, you are not in a playground. It is part of the intensity of the experience that you are out by yourself, far from any help. The beautiful thing about going into the real wild areas of the world is *you enter them on their terms*, and if you do not, they may wipe you out.

Years ago, I went on a twelve-day backpacking trip with a friend of mine, and the first evening I lit our stove, the line that connected it to the fuel bottle broke. We had all this food and no stove. In the Sierras, you are not supposed to make any open fires above 10,000 feet, and the trails we were on were mostly above 10,000 feet, so we had a dilemma. The funny thing is, this stove broke within a day's walk of our car, so we could have easily turned around and left, but we never talked about going back. I never considered the possibility of not doing this trip. When we got down to some lower areas, we started tiny campfires—just enough to cook some food, as we were trying to do as little damage as possible—and sometimes we ate our food uncooked. I remember on the last night, with about thirty-six hours to go, we were low on food. We had only one small box of cornbread mix, and we had no way to cook it, because we were camping at close to 12,000 feet so we could not burn anything (there was nothing up there to burn anyway). I was famished, as we had walked about eighteen miles that day, so I put the mix in a bowl, stirred some water into it, and drank the whole thing down. I drank an entire box of cornbread mix! It was awful, but the next day I was glad I did because we had another twenty miles to hike out.

Even though it tasted terrible, I actually enjoyed that raw cornmeal, because in that moment I was in a direct relationship with life on life's terms. As human beings, we get accustomed to bending everything to our comfort. Think about how much time and energy and money is spent on trying to make ourselves comfortable and fill our leisure time so we never have a moment of quietness. When you go into the mountains, you have none of that—you sleep on a half-inch-thick pad; it is freezing in the morning, even in the middle of the summer if you are higher than 10,000 feet; it is cold at night; you have to cook and wash all your dishes without a sink. You are having to conform to your environment constantly, almost every minute of the day, and if you do not, you could end up in big trouble fast.

This is what I have always loved about the mountains. There is no negotiating. The mountains make no effort to make us comfortable, and the beautiful thing is we find we do not need to be made comfortable. We can be tired, and our feet can be sore, and our hips can be painful, and we still pull the tent up, unpack everything, cook for ourselves, clean for ourselves, and pack it all up again in the morning. It is one task after another. Yet many people stay away from nature; they find the idea of backpacking horrendous. Who would want to do that? Who would want to sleep on the ground? To some, it sounds like purgatory at best.

It reminds me of when I first started to do retreats at Zen temples and monasteries. We were doing rigorous spiritual work, meditating for about fifteen periods a day and eating all our meals in meditation posture in the meditation hall, which added another three periods of sitting a day. One of the things I loved most is that those who ran that environment, that temple or retreat center, were not going to do anything to make my life easier. I had to fit into what they had established; otherwise I could go home. There was no negotiation.

I remember hearing the late Houn Jiyu-Kennett Roshi, who was the abbess of Shasta Abbey monastery in Mount Shasta, California, teach. She had done a lot of her Zen training at one of the biggest monasteries in Japan and was the first woman who ever went through it there, which was a difficult—at times even hellish—experience. She ended up becoming the first female to be sanctioned by the Soto School. Kennett Roshi told a wonderful story about the time a novice monk who had not been there long started to complain, although as nicely as he could, that he did not have enough room to sleep. In that monastery, you sleep where you meditate and eat; at night you put away your sitting cushion and roll out a thin mat. The novice approached the teacher, saying, "It seems a little confining for me. I need a little more space to sleep." The teacher said, "Oh? Why don't you lie down on the floor?" So the monk lay down on the floor, and the teacher took a piece of chalk and outlined his body. He put the mat on the top of the outline and said, "I have good news for you. You are smaller than the mat you are sleeping on. You have plenty of room. Good for you!"

That is not what the novice monk wanted to hear, but in a nice way he had been told, "This place is not changing for you, buddy. There is no room for your ego here." This is part of what I liked about those retreats, even though they were challenging. There is no negotiation; you must let go of this comfort principle that can so easily start to dominate your life. You realize you are in an environment that you must adapt to; the environment is not going to adapt itself to you. If you are backpacking high up in the mountains, you adapt, go home, or die. In a Zen temple, you either adapt yourself to the procedures of that temple or you go home. There is no use arguing with anybody about it, as the rules are not going to change for you, and if you are stuck in your ego, it can be very difficult. You can always find thirty ways that things can be improved, but in a Zen temple nobody is listening to you, mostly because they have heard it all.

I am not a guy who likes ritual, I am not a big "form" guy, and I am not an organized religion guy—Arvis, my main teacher, taught out of her living room—but one of the things I like about Zen retreats, like being in the mountains, is that it is a relief to let all that comfort seeking go and enter something else. Something deep inside you rejoices when it no longer has to be preoccupied all the time with, *How do I feel? Do I like it? Do I not like it? Is it right for me? Is it not right for me?* You go to the grocery store, for God's sake, and there are thirty different varieties of peanut butter to choose from. We may think, *Oh, how lucky am I? Thirty kinds of peanut butter to choose from when I go to the market.* But somebody in some other part of the world would love to have even one jar of peanut butter because they are starving to death, right? To them, thirty jars of peanut butter is ridiculous. Does having thirty kinds of peanut butter to choose from make us happier? Does it add enjoyment because we can spend that extra three or four minutes scratching our heads and wondering which peanut butter to buy?

My point is not whether we have a lot of choices or not; I am talking, not about those external things, but about our internal relationship with them. I found out that I could go into the mountains and leave behind that within me that is always analyzing and wondering, *How's this working for me, and is this as comfortable as I can make it, and is everything the way I want it?* I could be completely relieved of that and go into an environment where that game does not play, because nobody is listening. You can talk to the trees and suggest they move themselves to a different place because they keep getting in the way of where you want to walk, but the trees are not listening, and they are not going to move. You can either rail against that fact or let go. And as soon as you let go, it is as if every tree is in the perfect place. How did that happen? How did every tree know to grow in the perfect location? A minute ago, it all seemed to be haphazard and wrong, but now it seems to be divinely planned. It is a switch of perception, is it not? A change of orientation, a turning of the heart, a letting go.

In the West, we are focused on comfort. I live in a place called Los Gatos, which is one of the more beautiful little towns in the Silicon Valley, right up against the foothills. My wife, Mukti, and I were walking downtown one time, and we passed a store that sold mattresses; every mattress in this store was organic, made of special material, and the most highly engineered thing you could buy. I laughed. Do we need beds that are that perfect? We are all taught that comfort is what makes you happy and that getting everything you want or as much as you want or as much as you can get will make you happy. Having things go the way you want makes you happy. Having an infinite variety of choices of the same thing makes you happy. Right?

Do not misunderstand me; if I have the choices in front of me, I will take part, I will choose the one I want, and I will recognize the ridiculous good fortune of living in a place that offers this number of choices. I know we are not going to go back to three types of peanut butter—hell, there were more than three types of peanut butter when I was a kid, and that was a long time ago. In a way, this is why I am talking about being in the wilderness—because I think it is good for us. I do things occasionally to keep myself familiar with hunger, discomfort, and cold. I'll go out of my way at times to make myself less than comfortable, so that I do not lose contact with life.

I am aware that I am extremely privileged and can run back to being comfortable anytime I want, because this is the position that I am in and the country that I live in. We have an embarrassingly high proportion of people in poverty, but nonetheless we are an extraordinarily wealthy country. You walk into your house and you turn on your heat or your air conditioning; when it is dark you turn on the lights. But when you have things beyond your necessities, you are constantly managing life, which is why it can be beautiful to go back into the mountains and enter them on their terms. There is a freedom in that raw and direct experience of life. Out in the wilderness, when it gets dark, you go to bed. Even if you stay up reading a book with a flashlight, that battery is going to be gone soon, and you are going to have to go to sleep.

It is useful to reflect on what happiness is. I talk about deeper forms of satisfaction that are associated with spiritual awakening and revelation. On a more relative level, now and then do you take time—real time—to contemplate what makes you happy? It is nice to have comfortable things, and it is nice to reach in the refrigerator and pull out something yummy any darn time you want, but that is *pleasure*, that is not *happiness*. What makes you happy? What contributes to your happiness? What takes away from your happiness?

When we contemplate these questions in a deep way, they can bring us back to our senses, back to our center, back to our heart, and back to our being. We can return to loving the simple things and appreciating them. We can notice that we are happiest when we are contributing to the welfare of someone else; being a positive or benevolent presence in someone else's life is a great contributor to happiness.

Making ourselves comfortable at every second does not necessarily make us happy. This is what I have found when I have gone back to the mountains, which I do every year: there is a happiness that is an aspect of *being*. To be is itself happiness. Even beyond the bliss of pure being, what contributes to happiness, flourishing, love, and joy? The things that come to my mind are not the things that bring me the most ease and comfort. I find satisfaction in actions like contributing to the welfare of others, loving well, and connecting with nature.

There are so many kinds of intimate connection, are there not? There is the intimate connection we have with friends or lovers or family members. Sometimes you can meet a stranger as you are standing in line at the grocery store and have an intimate connection. On a deeper level, we can have an intimate connection with the truth of our being, with the sacred dimension of life, and with what we call "the world around us." The Zen master Dogen talked of enlightenment as an absolute intimacy with the ten thousand things. In Buddhism when they say, "the ten thousand things," they mean everything. What is enlightenment? An absolute intimacy with the ten thousand things. That is happiness.

For a spiritual teacher, seeing the joy on a person's face is wonderful. To witness someone take the next step in their own evolution—maybe it is a leap, maybe it is tiny—is a beautiful thing. There are things that contribute to happiness—ours and others'—and it is good to reflect on them and not assume we know. When we reflect, we can ask, *Oh, how much of my energy, of my life-force, am I putting into what makes me happy?* Contemplate what contributes to your happiness. You might be surprised by some of the things you find.

It can be interesting to see how you contribute to the happiness of others. Not asking, *How* should *I?*—do not turn it into a big guilt trip—but asking, *How* do *I?* I do not think we need to be told what makes us happy, nor do I think we need to be told what makes others happy; rather, we need to be quiet and contemplate what nourishes happiness. The things that make people happy touch the human heart and the human soul.

You have activities that will move you or awaken a sense of sacredness, and they may not involve traipsing off into the mountains. What are yours? What is the thing that helps you reconnect? How much time do you spend doing it? Contemplate that, because you might find the means to your well-being and the well-being of others is a lot closer than you imagine. That is when all these elements start to come together—happiness, well-being, love, and compassion—and you start to feel they are just different ways of speaking, living, and experiencing the same thing.

Pristine Buddha Mind

IT IS THE NOTHING IN WHICH EVERYTHING OCCURS.

Exploring subjective experience means exploring the experience you are having right now and what it is that is having the experience. In spirituality, we are taught that one of the problems we share—the reason we suffer, the reason we do not perceive the world or ourselves as a unified whole—is that our mind is conditioned, our body is conditioned, and therefore the way we perceive and experience life is also conditioned, which is true. A lot of the thinking is, *If we could uncondition the mind enough, then we could awaken or reach enlightenment.* So spiritual practitioners diligently try to eliminate as much conditioning as they can. Whether you are trying to do this or not, there is a part of your being, and of consciousness, that is unnoticed—that is the pristine nature of consciousness.

If you look, you will realize that everyone's mind and thoughts are conditioned. A lot of the conditioning is useless; a lot of it leads to misunderstanding, suffering, fear, anger, or violence. There is also garden-variety conditioning that is like computer programming, which causes your heart to beat and your lungs to breathe without you having to think about it or even understand how it happens. However, there is also an aspect of consciousness in everybody and in everything that is unconditioned. No matter how conditioned you are, the most essential aspect of consciousness is unconditioned and will always remain pristine. Put simply, the consciousness that is aware of the conditioned nature of your mind, body, and even the conditioned nature of consciousness is itself unconditioned. You are perceiving this moment—right now—with unconditioned consciousness, or pristine consciousness. It is the experience of noticing that your mind is talking to itself in an infinity of quiet space, so no matter how much your mind talks to itself, it is talking to itself from within silence. Every word that arises in your mind arises in a wordless consciousness, and every feeling is felt by something that is not a feeling.

It is said you cannot hear your hearing, nor taste your tasting, nor touch your touching, just as you cannot physically grab any of these ways of perceiving. Consider hearing: we hear in a conditioned way. Everything that we hear goes through the matrix of the mind, and as it does, our mind is telling us whether it is pleasant or unpleasant, whether we like it or do not like it, agree with it or do not agree with it, and so on. Yet even as that is happening, it is happening within a prior state of consciousness that is unconditioned and egoless. The ego exists within an egoless state in the same way that the noise of thinking exists within a quiet, wordless space.

I am writing from direct experience right now, experience that anybody can look at and have; I am not espousing profound philosophical theory. We can try to uncondition ourselves forever, but the problem is that we keep acquiring conditioning as fast as we get rid of it. We can try to uncondition ourselves, or we can notice that the ground of our consciousness is already unconditioned. Conditioning can arise within it, and it can play itself out within it, but the ground of consciousness is itself unconditioned. In Buddhist terms, it is the pristine Buddha mind—not the thinking mind, not the conceptualizing mind—in which those conceptualizations occur and in which conditioning may arise and be experienced and felt. In Sanskrit the word *buddha* means "awakened" or "enlightened." It is like your awareness is buddha in this sense.

This is hard for us to perceive as long as we are trying to change any part of our experience. We are used to trying to change our experience all the time; we are not so used to leaving our experience alone. If we leave our experience alone with all our perceptions—without interpreting them, without imagining they are right or wrong or conditioned or not—if we leave everything alone, then we begin to intuit that the nature of consciousness, the nature of awareness, is like the space and the sky: unobstructed. It is nothing, but it is the nothing in which everything occurs. We should be careful with that kind of a statement, though—that the ultimate nature of awareness is pristine and that it is that in which everything occurs—because our mind might then think that it is *other* than what occurs. The pristine, pure nature of conscious awareness does not become pure at any point in time; it already is. Even if some impurity or distorted, conditioned viewpoint arises within it, it itself is not distorted—but neither is it separate or other than what arises.

Everything that arises, that is experienced, felt, known, and perceived, begins within consciousness. There is no such thing as an experience for you to have that does not arise within conscious awareness. If everything always arises within conscious awareness—whether you recognize it or not—then nothing can be separate and other than conscious awareness, because you never find them existing apart from each other.

I understand that it is easy to become philosophical and ask all sorts of interesting questions about the nature of reality based on what I have said, but for the moment I do not want to get into the deeper philosophical debates about whether something exists without you being conscious of it. Some schools of spirituality would say that no, nothing exists until that moment that you are aware of it, and other schools would say something different; but that is not a debate I am going to have right now. What I want to point out is that right now, at this instant, whatever is within your consciousness is by necessity conditioned (to some extent) by the consciousness that is aware of this moment. The consciousness that is aware of the conditioning is not itself conditioned.

I am pushing the boundaries of language here—stating that the nature of consciousness can be conditioned and unconditioned simultaneously—but if you notice that, then the very act of noticing itself is pure and unconditioned. The secondary act—of thinking about what you notice or see or hear, analyzing it, and describing it to yourself or somebody else—is conditioned. Conditioning does not always mean "bad," as conditioning is beating your heart right now and is firing your neurons. There is much talk in spiritual circles about how our personal conditioning creates chaos, suffering, anger, and upset, and so we tend to think of conditioning only in a negative sense, but as I mentioned earlier, there is a whole host of conditioning that is positive. Most of what is happening in your brain right now to help give you the experience of this moment is happening all by itself, because it is conditioned—it is programmed.

There was a seventeenth-century Zen master named Bankei Yotaku. While he was a seeker, he tried to meditate night and day, until his legs nearly atrophied and he almost died of tuberculosis. At about the time he was going to die, he had a great awakening. He called this "the unborn Buddha mind" and pointed out that the simple things—like hearing and knowing what we hear—occur because of this unborn Buddha mind. What we hear may be conditioned, but the unborn Buddha mind is not; what you see may be conditioned, may depend on its entire environment for its existence and therefore is conditioned by its environment, but the unborn Buddha mind is not.

I am not saying that consciousness is separate from the environment at all, because it is not, but for the sake of this investigation, try to see how unconditioned your consciousness is—not the thoughts that float around in your consciousness, not the feelings that arise within your consciousness, but consciousness or awareness itself. You can think yourself into the environment of what I am talking about, but when we come to realize and see that there is an unconditioned nature of our being, that it is pristine, in that sense it is a Buddha mind. This unconditioned, pristine Buddha mind exists within everyone.

I am not suggesting that you try to hole up in this Buddha mind, hide from all your conditioning, or any of that sort of nonsense. A great amount of healing can occur when the conditioned aspect of your being interacts in a conscious and knowing way with the unconditioned nature of consciousness. When the conditioned and the unconditioned meet in a conscious way, it is a tremendously powerful solvent to unnecessary conditioning. Seeing the conditioned and the unconditioned as two things is like seeing something from heads or tails: from one side, it is conditioned, but flip it over, and it is unconditioned. However, when we bring our awareness to it, then there is another element: we are conscious of what is happening.

To be conscious of consciousness is different from being unconscious of consciousness. To be conscious of the pristine nature of the ground of your conscious being—of your Buddha mind—is a profoundly different state of being to exist within than knowing only the conditioned nature of your being. It is not about having one or the other; it is about seeing both the heads and tails of the same thing. When you are conscious of the *conditioned* nature of your being and you are conscious of the *unconditioned* nature of your being, an interaction and a transformation happen because consciousness is throughout the whole of it.

Something tremendously liberating occurs when the unconditioned meets that which is conditioned—in not preferring one over the other, not grasping at the unconditioned and pushing away the conditioned, but seeing that they exist simultaneously. It is amazing to see that from the beginning there was an aspect of consciousness, an aspect of awareness that was pristine, that was unconditioned and remains so always. It is transformational because you are then including much more of your being within your conscious recognition. I am not talking about what you are *aware of*, but about the nature of your awareness itself: it is already clear, unconditioned, and free, because there are not any ideas to distort it. As soon as you grab onto an idea, that idea starts to condition your consciousness—to condition the way you see things, the way you feel about them, and the way you think about them.

Even while that conditioning process is happening and unfolding, it is doing so within pristine Buddha nature, within the unconditioned nature of consciousness or awareness. This is mind-blowingly simple. Once you see it, you wonder how you ever did *not* see it, because it is not hidden; there is nothing obscure about it and no amount of complicated thinking that helps you get there. Simply put, for this moment, you are not floating in the conceptual current. The mind may be talking to itself, but it is talking to itself within a space that is not talking.

Think of consciousness as a space for whatever is. Imagine you go to a symphony hall. If there is no symphony, it is quiet. If they have a symphony, there is music; but the symphony can be heard only because it is quiet in the room even when there is noise in the room. I know that is hard to understand, because I am going translogical on you for a moment: *How can there be sound and no sound?* Pause and look at it. If there were no silence for sound to happen within, there would be no sound—they go together. A rock 'n' roll band can come into the symphony hall and play, and suddenly the walls are shaking with the sound of the music, but it does not change the nature of the space—the space is the same space whether it is filled with noise, good rock 'n' roll, bad rock 'n' roll, good symphony music, jazz, or no sound. The nature of the space in the room is like the nature of the sky—clouds come, clouds go, snow comes and goes, but the sky has its own purity and its own way of being unobstructed. This is why the sky is used as a metaphor for the unconditioned nature of consciousness, because it is already there and because no matter what is going on within the sky—or within consciousness—it still remains as pure as it ever was. Clouds and snow are things that exist within the space of the sky, not truly obscuring the sky at all.

The sky and the symphony hall are metaphors for our most immediate experience and our most immediate perception of being. The most immediate one is unconditioned silence—a silence like when our mind stops talking to itself. Then there is another silence, a subtler and more foundational silence, which is the silence in which your mind is talking to itself. However, the silence in which your mind is talking to itself is still silent; it is still itself even when your mind is talking within it and creating noise. We are always thinking in dualistic terms—silent or not silent, noise or no noise—but the description of things is not the way things are. There can be both silence and sound: there can be no sound without silence, and when there is sound there is still silence. Even to say this is counterintuitive.

If we do not think that reality needs to conform to our dualistic ideas about reality, then we can pay attention to the way things are, rather than the way we have conceptualized them. That is where we might run into the pristine Buddha mind—the consciousness that is always quiet, always awake, always present, and always there. It is not an experience, but it is the space in which experiences arise. Therefore, it is not *other* than experience, and it is not separate. To recognize that is life changing and also beneficial, as it becomes a safe space for the conditioning that does not work well or is not true to unfurl itself. There can be a transformation through the sensing of the interaction of the conditioned and the unconditioned, subtle or obvious, pristine nature of your consciousness.

Being Still

Think about these two words: *being still.* Not *"Be* still," which can sound more like a directive, like something you are supposed to do—*"Be still!"* But *being still* is different. It is not a command, and it implies there is something happening right now, something called "stillness," that we can be. "Be still" can be interpreted as, *Uh-oh, there is something I have got to do. I have got to be still, and I may or may not be good at that.* But "being" is not telling you to do or not do something.

What does being still mean for you? Even speaking the words leads one to experience a stillness. We are not trying to be still, and we are not taking the words as an instruction or something we must do. The phrase is more imaginative; it is a little whisper that occasionally floats through the mind . . . being still. It is a way of drawing attention to stillness, rather than suggesting that we try to do stillness, and that's a big difference. It may seem subtle at first, but I would suggest that it is not. Just like pristine Buddha mind that already exists, "being still" is something you can become aware of and something you notice. Notice being still.

It is funny that in the human world we can have trouble finding a place where we human *beings* are being still in any recognizable way. We are a noisy species, and I may be contributing to some of that noise right now with my words. When we get out in the natural environment or any environment where there are not a lot of people making noise, it is amazing how much of life is still and quiet, and it is amazing, within that stillness and that quiet, how much being there is.

A big part of spirituality is exploring the nature of being and exploring the nature of existing. *What is it to exist? What is it to be? Who am I?* These questions delve into the mystery of being. There is something about everyone we ever meet that falls into this category of what I am calling "being"—some aspect of them that is not defined by their occupation, by what religion they adhere to, by their family history, or by their hopes for the future. There is something more immediate than that when you meet somebody, and what you are meeting is their being. It is something that we habitually discount, because being is not conceptual. We can talk about our work, we can talk about interests, we can talk about what we like and what we do not like, but with being or existing, there is not much to talk about—at least on the surface. As we go deeper, we see that being is the essential mystery of our existence. What does it mean when we say, "I am"? "I am" is itself incredible mystery.

Spirituality is, at the end of the day, the exploration of being; it is the exploration of our experience, our perception of being, of existing, of our self, of our life, and not only of ours, but of the nature of existence itself. Being is tough to conceptualize, but every time we meet each other, we meet being; every time we interact with any part of life, which we are doing right now, we must be in order to do that. What is the nature of your being or your existing? What are you at the level of being? What are you at that profound and most fundamental level? You were being before you had language, as a newborn baby is being. Infants have their full complement of being, even though they are not thinking a single word and even though we have not taught them anything yet. As soon as we learn words and language, they envelop our being, and we become mesmerized by what we say.

I try my best not to be mesmerized by what I say. I am trying to communicate something that is not the word, that is not language, but that is immediate, instantaneous, and intuitive understanding. If we are caught too much in the conceptual mind, we will lose sight of our insight. Even though I am using concepts right now to explain this to you and you are using concepts to understand what I am writing, there is something more fundamental. Any conscious moment is a moment of being. We are having those moments when we feel the spontaneous and natural enjoyment or bliss of being and existing, in any form whatsoever, and to be—to exist—is itself blissful and beautiful. What happens within that existence is sometimes experienced as beautiful, and sometimes the experience is anything but beautiful, but we are not taught to pay much attention to the basic act of existing. We are taught to pay attention to our self-image and our idea of ourselves: *Am I spiritual enough? Am I a materialist? Am I talented or not talented? How good do I look? What do I do for my occupation? What are my interests?* When we are trying to describe ourselves to somebody, we are referring to all these things. The funny part is that the core of our existence is the fundamental experience of being and of existing, yet words cannot fully communicate what it is to be.

I am sure there are people who go their whole life without pondering this for a split second. I do not happen to be one of them; I am one of those people who has always felt the experience of being to be amazing in its mystery. I do not mean it always feels good, as sometimes being feels terrible, but the pure experience of being itself is freedom. Not being this or that, not being something that you can describe through what you have done or like or dislike or whatever, but the sheer act of existence is an astounding miracle.

When I say "miracle," I am not whitewashing all the difficulties that happen in life. However, throughout it all is the experience of being. I am not making being into a thing; I am not saying, "There is this thing inside you called 'being,'" as if you have a secret essence. Being is a simple thing; it is the sheer act of existing. In that sense, being and consciousness are the same thing. To be is to be conscious in some way and to experience the miracle of being. That there is anything instead of nothing itself takes consciousness, takes an awareness, so "being" is synonymous with "awareness" or "consciousness." We desire being. We desire the bliss of being, the freedom of it, and the joy of letting go into being—not being this, or being that, or being someone, or being nothing, or however you would define it, but being.

Meditation is the art of being. Unfortunately, we turn it into the art of doing. We ask, *What am I doing? I am meditating. Well, what is that? Well, I am trying to be.* Sometimes we introduce too much unnecessary struggle or a strife that does not need to be part of it. Meditation is the art of being still, to be, and you do not have to do anything to be—you are, and I am. Nothing is required for you to be. "I am" requires nothing more, and there is no need to define beyond that. *I am good, I am bad, I am right, I am wrong*—those thoughts are part of life as well, but none of that defines being. The sheer act of existence, the sheer act of being and of consciousness, is its own miracle.

Being, consciousness, truth, bliss, the Sanskrit word *satchitananda* . . . when we get down to experience, it is being in a conscious way instead of an unconscious way and to knowingly be instead of falling asleep at the wheel, driven by impulse and conditioning. We are still being then, but we are being in an unconscious way. That is why in spirituality we use the word "awakening": awakening means we are no longer asleep at the wheel. Yes, if we are asleep we are still being, but we are being in an unconscious manner, with the sheer brute force of conditioning playing itself out through our entire life. We can be in that way, but it happens to be unsatisfactory.

A lot of sorrow arises if conditioned being is as far as we ever take being, yet sadly, that is about as far as most people go in their exploration. However, to be is to be conscious, to be without trying to be this or that, and to experience the ground of your being, which gives rise to bliss. These aspects of true nature are not always clear, especially when we are lost in the conceptual mind or the emotional body. Those are two reference points where people hang out, as some people are conceptually oriented and others are emotionally oriented. Both have their strengths and their weaknesses, but I am not looking at being from a conceptual or an emotional position. Being is something more primary and more fundamental.

Being is the real foundational nature of what we are. It sounds paradoxical—we are everything and nothing—but in all of that, we are the pristine Buddha mind, the pure unconditioned consciousness, and we are also the total environment. This means we are one with everything, which is not one *with* everything, because we *are* everything. So we are everything, and we are nothing, and whatever word we want to give to that, we are also being—we are being nothing, we are being everything. The sheer act of being itself, of existing, is the most fundamental understanding of "I am." No definition, no *I am this, I am that, I am good, I am bad, I am right, I am wrong, I am spiritual, I am unspiritual, I am enlightened, I am unenlightened.* All of that is the world of description, but prior to the world of description is "I am," and even before that, there is being. In being there is no tension, and there is no anxiety or fear or evaluation; there is pure presence, pure existence, and pure being still.

It is important not to overdescribe the indescribable, but instead to bridge the gap between descriptions, as strong or weak as they may be, to reach your deepest and most direct experience of being—the bliss, the clarity, and the profound sense of "all is well." When we are connected to this, we have a new foundation from which to live life and meet challenges.

Exploring Birth, Life, and Death

AT NO MOMENT IS THE WAVE SOMETHING OTHER
THAN THE OCEAN, AND AT NO MOMENT IS THE OCEAN
SOMETHING OTHER THAN THE WAVE.

Our entire existence is all about birth, the living of life, and then the eventual culmination in death. All three of these processes can be encountered in a variety of ways—with wonderment and joy, as suffering and torment, as relief and peace; they run the whole gamut of the human experience. We may assume that we are involved only in the living part, but all three of these stages go together—you can't have one without the other two.

I want to forewarn you here that I am going to be getting underneath the conventional views of birth, life, and death; if we are going to take a profound look at these things, we should almost expect that we are going to approach them from an unconventional perspective. In this sense, "an unconventional perspective" means from the viewpoint of awakened consciousness.

We think of birth, life, and death as sequential: our terrestrial life begins at birth and concludes at death. From this conventional perspective, it is hard to argue with the reality of experiencing those things. We experience birth when we are born, we experience life when we are alive, and then in the conventional sense we think of the end of our life as death. Zen Buddhism teaches us that the Great Matter, the whole reason for meditation and spiritual practice, is to solve the question of birth, life, and death. That is a big task to undertake. Instead of "solve," think of it as "resolve," because "solving" implies that we are done with it—we have found the answer and it has some finality. But even if we "resolve" something, we still are going through it, and the word does not necessarily imply an ending.

The quest for enlightenment is all about extraordinarily deep observation and about being curious toward our current experience. Many of us think that the search for enlightenment is a quest for an experience that is not now present, something that might be called "an enlightenment experience," but it is important to realize that that is a misunderstanding of what enlightenment is all about and of what opens the door for the grace of enlightenment to dawn within us. We do not find enlightenment because we are looking for a particular experience called "enlightenment." Enlightenment reveals itself through the exploration of our current experience. It does not matter what our current experience is, because the exploration of the experience is the exploration of the nature of experience and of the so-called experiencer—they are one and the same.

Enlightenment or awakening is like cracking the nut of experience; it is like opening our experience in a vast, deep way, but it involves an intense, focused attention on the present moment of experience. Enlightenment is not to be found by shopping for a different experience or by trying to change your current experience. The act of looking into the nature of your birth and death, of observing it, will affect your experience of it. It will begin to change your experience in a positive way, because it feels better to become more conscious. However, even though our experience changes through the act of observing it, enlightenment is not the search for a changed experience. Even though enlightenment will change our experience and our perception of the present moment, if we approach it as if we are looking for a change, then we are missing what the way, the path, and the method are.

We should think about how to engage with this spiritual yearning. We may use the word "enlightenment," we may use the word "freedom," or "unity," or "the mystery of God"—there are many different terminologies that we can use—but fundamentally we are all interested in the true nature of our current experience of being. In other words: *What are we? What am I? What is this world? What is birth? What is life? What is death?* What are these phenomena beyond what we have been taught and beyond our conventional understanding? Our conventional understanding does not help us. Our conventional ways of understanding birth, life, and death end up confusing us and eventually creating more tension, anxiety, fear, and suffering than is necessary.

Try to connect these statements intuitively to your experience. That does not mean you are going to be experiencing everything exactly as I am describing it, but I would not want you to read this as though it is a textbook filled with so much information you are acquiring or taking in—that is a misunderstanding of what dharma is all about. What Buddhists call "dharma," or spiritual truth, is not something that we can learn. It is not like sitting down and listening to a lecture on biology or chemistry or physics and then learning more about biology, about chemistry, and about how to solve equations of physics. In spirituality, we are endeavoring to go beyond mere information, beyond the collecting of ideas and concepts and theoretical forms of understanding. If you fathom these basics about how to approach spirituality, then you will waste far less time.

When I say, "You will waste far less time," I mean this whole endeavor of solving or resolving the Great Matter of birth, life, and death can take you years and years less—if not decades and decades less, if not lifetimes less—if you comprehend how to approach it. If we do not know how to approach it, then it becomes like somebody handing you an instrument and saying, "Okay, go learn how to play this." You can make sounds and find notes, but creating music almost always takes a certain amount of direction. It is essential if you are to learn how to play an instrument, and if you are going to make the best use of your time and become the best musician you can be, that you know how to practice. You do not just blow into the thing and hope music starts to come out; there is a prescribed technique of how to play an instrument. Even though spirituality is not equivalent to learning how to do something, it is important that we at least understand the basic approach that has guided other spiritual seekers.

The basic approach in this instance is for a moment to let go of seeking something outside of your current experience. You may or may not like your current experience, but either way, it is about the deep exploration into the right here and right now. That is what spirituality is, and that is what spiritual disciplines are for. It is important to understand what they are for; otherwise you might use them to chase something in the future, which will cause you to do nothing but go around in circles, like a dog when it chases its tail.

To explore birth, life, and death, we ask, "What are we?" Again, what I am going to give you here are words, but remember, I am trying to present the most accurate words I can for how I perceive things. If we do not mistake the description for what I am describing, then perhaps the words will be useful. It is like going to a restaurant and not confusing the menu for the meal; the menu helps you to orient and tell the server what meal you want, but the menu will not satisfy your hunger, and it will not give you the nutrients that your body craves and needs. So it is with a teaching like this one. My words are like the menu, but the meal is going to be found within your individual experience. My suggestion is to intuitively feel into and to sit with what I am saying, however it presents itself in you.

Generally, our conventional view of ourselves—of anything, actually, but in this case, ourselves—is simple. We think that we are limited to the outside edge of our skin and that we are somehow contained within our body; intuitively there is a sense that somehow "I am in here, whatever I am," that there is an "I," there is a "me," and it is in my body. Most people when asked to intuitively sense where their self is within the body say it is somewhere behind the eyes. It is as if there is a sense—not a reality, but a sense—of some little man or little woman or ego structure that is inside of you, and it is operating your body and experiencing life through it. You may have a belief that you are pure spirit or pure consciousness or whatever you want to label it, and if you experience that, then that is a whole other matter, but what I am addressing here is how the average person experiences themselves.

If we look at it from a deeper level, most of us experience ourselves primarily through the way the mind talks to itself—the way your mind talks to you about you—and that is fueled and generated by memory. Imagine if you suddenly had zero memory, so that if you looked back to who you were in the past, there would be no childhood, no adolescence, and no reference—not even to five minutes ago, not even to one minute ago—no memory of anything that came before now. Can you see how you would not even know who you were? That is how much we rely on memory from the ego perspective. It happens unconsciously. We do not sit around saying, "I am going to remember myself," but memory is stored in our brain cells, and it is the filter through which we view every moment; it colors every action and every experience. Our experiences are filtered through the past, but if you envision that there is no past—if you somehow plopped down wherever you are, as if you just suddenly arrived on planet Earth—who or what would you be?

If there were no memory and suddenly you became conscious, it might feel like, *Wow, where am I?* because you would have no reference point or history to tell you where you are, to tell you if you are in your house, or if the watch you are wearing belongs to you, or where you got the clothes on your back. Contemplating this helps us get a feel for how much our sense of self is derived through memory, from the past. It happens so automatically that we are not aware of the process, but nonetheless, this is our more internalized sense of who we are. To say that it is deriving itself from the past is also a way of saying that it is deriving itself from our conditioning, because the past is what conditions us to have certain opinions and to feel specific ways about certain events. However, if you had no memory whatsoever, you would not experience yourself as your everyday ideas and feelings about yourself; you would have nothing with which to generate a self.

Sometimes when people get an intuitive glimmer of what I am talking about here, they experience a combination of thrill and fear. It is as if to say, "Wow, there is freedom!" because we are relieved of the psychological baggage, which is contained and carried into the present moment through memory. If you had no baggage, all the troubles that you had from yesterday and every day before that would suddenly be gone; life would begin anew in this instant, at least as far as you were concerned, because you would not be able to remember the previous instant.

I am painting this picture so you can see the flimsiness of our conventional sense of self derived through memory. It is not something that has much at all to do with the present moment. When we start to examine our true nature and when we start to ask, "What am I?" we start to peer beyond our identifications with the past. All of memory is stored in our minds through images and thoughts and feelings. If we look, it does not take long to see that I am not a thought, and neither are you. Another way to understand this is to flip it around and look from the ego's point of view: *I am only derived.* The ego is only derived through thoughts and memory and whatever the current feeling state is. That is how it constructs itself from moment to moment; it is created every instant through memory, the act of self-talk, and the feelings that that self-talk and memory generate.

That is a basic way of explaining what is constructing our sense of the ego self. It intuitively feels like, *I am in here somewhere*—somewhere in your head or in your body. *I am in here and I am operating this thing*—as if the body were a car and you were in the driver's seat. However, when we examine that, it quickly starts to break down. We start to see that the way we have been taught to reference ourselves and who we are is derived through our thinking and feeling and memory.

Even when we are not engaged in a conscious act of memory, when we are not thinking—and with meditation practice we can begin to notice moments when we are not thinking—we do not disappear in a puff of smoke; something about us still is. It is fascinating if you start to explore it. We notice that when we give anything a name—like "tree" or "car" or "cloud" or "piece of paper" or the name given to you at birth—we adopt a conditioned way of viewing that named thing. We see our body as this object that moves through space and time, as it walks on the earth and moves through the air. However, if you look at your body, you notice that every part of it is connected to its environment. Usually we think, *I am not the air. I need air, but I am not air*, but would you even exist without air to breathe? Would you exist without water? And where does water come from? The clouds, the streams, the rivers, the rain, and the elements that make up your whole body are all found within our environment, or what we call "the outside world." Every aspect of the body depends on the outside world; it is entirely a product of the environment.

We have this feeling, because we have been taught it, that "I" am contained within a body, that "my" body is a discrete object that walks around in the world and that moves through life. But when we start to examine it, we realize that this notion and the intuitive feeling that goes along with it are illusory. We realize that—as I often say when I'm teaching and have said earlier in this book—we *are* our environment. We do not exist without our environment; we would not exist if there were no rain, if there were no minerals stored in the rocks, or if there were no food. Every part of our body-mind is a product of the environment; take the environment away, and there is no such thing as a body-mind.

The conventional way that we define things creates boundaries, as if any one thing is different or separate from its environment. This is why, when we have profound spiritual openings or realizations, the constructs of boundaries disappear, and we feel ourselves to be the entirety and to be whole. This is the experience of unity or of oneness or of no boundary. We know that we are the total environment and that the total environment is simultaneously appearing right now as a particular body. It is taking our form, and it is taking all the forms we see. It is not that we lose our particular body, but our particular body is the universe, in the same way that if you look at your hand, your hand is connected to your arm, which is connected to your shoulder, which is connected to your chest, which is connected to all the rest of your body. We can say that a hand is different from an elbow or it is different from a shoulder, and at times it can be helpful to think that, but as soon as we do, we start to think and feel and even perceive the hand as an abstract thing. The concept of your hand ends at your wrist, but an actual hand always includes a wrist and an arm, which includes a whole body. If your hand were to recognize the totality of what it is, it would not be something that begins at your wrist; that is an idea. Sometimes those ideas of things come in handy, but they are not true.

The boundaries names give to things are illusions; there are not boundaries, because everything runs into everything else, just like birth, life, and death. In the deep state of realization, we recognize that everything is everything else. We suddenly break through the way our concepts distort our perception and therefore our experience, and we intuit that a single grain of sand takes an entire universe.

Therefore, in a profound sense, a single grain of sand *is* the universe, and the universe is a single grain of sand. It is the same thing; the boundary lines are purely conceptual.

In deep spiritual experience, the boundary lines fall away, and we have a boundless—or, more accurately speaking, a boundaryless—experience of being. This brings an extraordinary sense of freedom and well-being and intimacy with the total environment and with our oneness with all things. These are not just nice-sounding spiritual platitudes or simple or fancy concepts that one is supposed either to agree or to disagree with; they are attempts to give words to actual perception, to recognize existence in a particular way—in a truer way. The ego mind is created through memory and concepts, and concepts by their nature create boundaries, because every time we call something a name, it is relevant only in relationship to what it *is not*. As I have said, part of awakening is to begin to see and experience life directly, not through all these boundaries that are created by language and memory. Deep spiritual revelation shows us that we are not separate from all that is, that life itself has no beginning or end, and that it is always changing forms. Water turns into a vapor or steam, falls to the ground, gets cold, becomes ice, gets heated up, melts, turns into a gas, and so it goes. A tree falls in the forest, and its elements decay back into the ground, releasing nutrients and giving rise to new trees and new elements, and the new trees fall, and life does not end; energy is conserved, life changes form, and there is never more or less of it.

If we are identified with a particular form, then we will experience this thing called death as the ultimate threat—in other words, the end of "me." What you are believing is this: *I so identify with life appearing in this particular way*—the way you look in the mirror when you wake up in the morning—*and death is going to be the end of that form; therefore it is going to be the end of me.* If that is how we are identified and if that is how we experience life, we are going to be afraid of death, because we are going to experience it as the end of us. In a real sense it will be, because the ego self does not survive death and the transformation of form. When life changes form—which is what death is—nothing about the life, the suchness of that being, even the physical body, goes anywhere; it does not disappear, but it changes form. Someone might say, "Well, that is a nice spiritual or religious idea to have and comfort yourself with," but remember, I am not talking about ideas. I am well aware that to merely believe what I am teaching here is of little to no use at all. If you believe it, that belief may well get in the way of experiencing it, because you will hold on to the belief and not bother with the deep experience.

I am not talking about a comforting philosophy or idea; I am talking about a completely different way to experience life from moment to moment. When we get this at a deep and fundamental level, we realize that there is no birth or death, because we do not somehow show up from nothing and become someone only to disappear into nothing again—that is an impossibility. Life takes a form, *boom!* There is a baby where there was not one before, and throughout its whole existence it is changing: it is growing up, then as it gets old enough, it starts to "grow down" again or to shrink. Even our own body, which we think is so stable, is in a constant process of change; the cells are continually dying, which means they are changing form, and new ones are coming into being, and that is a way of changing form as well.

If we equate ourselves with the ego mind, then, yes, death is a real thing, but if we awaken to the all-ness of existence—if we no longer see ourselves as separate from it—then death is not the end of anything except of life taking that particular form. Sometimes we will grieve because we loved life showing up as a certain person, and what I am examining here now is not a denial of that; sometimes when life changes its form and is no longer in the shape of our friend or our brother or our lover, we experience absence and grief and pain. Understanding the Great Matter of birth, life, and death is not a denial that change happens. It is seeing that existence, life as such, is in a constant state of change, but when it changes form there is no lessening of life whatsoever. If we are identified with the whole, then we understand that we do not come into being at this moment called birth, nor do we cease being at the moment called death. There will be fundamental and radical changes that life undergoes; birth is a radical change of form that life took, and death is a radical change too, as life is no longer in that known form. This understanding I am getting at is not the denial of change. What I am pointing to here is a deeper realization of "What am I?" A crucial part of spiritual growth or enlightenment is waking up from the hallucination of boundaries.

Practice recognizing how language—every word that you or I speak—imposes these boundaries upon things; to give something a name is to cut it off from its environment. As soon as you name something, it is as if you have taken a pencil and outlined that object according to how you have defined it. If you defined it a different way, the outline would change. But life does not have these outlines. One thing does not exist on one side of the line and another thing on the other side of the line; there is a continuum. Even though a tree looks different from a flower and a human being looks different from a dog, and even though life takes an infinite variety of forms, shapes, colors, textures, and personalities, remember that it is all life. It is like the ocean taking the innumerable forms of different waves, but at no moment is the wave something other than the ocean, and at no moment is the ocean something other than the wave. As soon as we say the word "wave," it is as if a wave is this thing that floats upon the top of the ocean. Our boundaries define the wave as if it exists separately in a way it does not and cannot.

Look at how the habit of naming things seems to cut them off from their environment, although whatever you are naming never exists independent of an environment. Your body does not exist independent of the environment. Your birth does not happen independent from your death. In a deep sense, the universe is an extension of your true body, and your body is a form that the universe is now taking. Sit with that, ponder it with ease, and wonder at it, like a child, with curiosity and with a gentleness of mind and a sensitivity of body.

You Are the Buddha

YOUR FORM WILL GO OUT OF BEING—WITH OR
WITHOUT REALIZATION—BUT THE REALITY OF YOU
DOES NOT COME INTO OR GO OUT OF ANYTHING.

Saying that the whole practice of Zen is to solve—or resolve—the Great Matter of birth, life, and death is a tall order. This reckoning, this coming to peace with birth, life, and death as the various forms that the single reality of you takes, is (at least in part) what it means to spiritually awaken and to be enlightened. We can all be assured that if nothing else, we human beings have birth, life, and death in common.

Let's start with the experience of birth. It is a definitive experience, not only for those of us who are being born but for the mothers who are birthing us. The act of birth defines mother and it defines child. As we know, Zen teachers often use koans, or existential questions, as teaching tools. A lot of these questions are worded in such a way that they tie your conceptual hands behind your back in the hope that you will fall into revelation or awakening, fall into direct experience rather than experience that has been adapted and distorted by your understanding, by the past, or by the ideas that you have in your mind. One often-used koan asks: "Who were you before your mother was born? Who were you before your parents were born?" With a question like that, one could easily start waxing philosophical: *Let me imagine, well . . . if I was pure spirit, then I was pure spirit or pure consciousness floating in the void of timelessness, and then my parents had a good and exciting night and . . .* boom! *I was thrust into the womb of my mother, only to be thrust into this event called life.* If you take your metaphysical speculation to a Zen master, you are going to get a conceptual, if not a literal, smack on the head as a way of saying, "Come on, get over that. You are still looking at things through concepts, through your ideas, and through your descriptions." The description is not what is described; your description of something is far, far away from whatever the thing you are describing is. Remember: *do not mistake the menu for the meal.* That seems obvious when you go to a restaurant, but in the other 99 percent of life, that is exactly what we human beings are doing. We have substituted our descriptions of ourselves and the world around us and of everything—God, reality, life, each other—and we have forgotten that our descriptions of things have almost nothing to do with the things themselves.

If we could only get that one point! We resist, even though it is so obvious when you sit with it that the description of something has almost nothing to do with whatever we are describing. The description of what it is like to drink a cup of water does not create the experience of what it is like to drink a cup of water—it does not produce the coolness of water, it does not produce the liquidity of water, it does not create the flow of water, and it does not create the feeling of having your thirst quenched. The most sophisticated description of something as simple as water cannot do any of those things, can it? Yet look at our lives: we are endlessly mistaking our descriptions of things for the things themselves, and so we divorce ourselves from reality and from our direct experience. That leads to a sense of isolation and of alienation.

It is like being in a prison where you can see life outside the prison walls through a window, but the only connection you have with it is a recording of somebody describing what it is like on the other side of that wall—the sunshine, the trees, the birds, the rain, the texture of the landscape—and so you feel an alienation from yourself, from others, and from life. The intellectual thinks, *If I got a better description of things, I would not feel so alienated.* Believe me, I love great and exact and beautiful descriptions of things—it is a lot of what I try to create when I teach—and I can appreciate the creativity and the artistry and the usefulness of them, but I try never to mistake the description of anything for the direct experience.

The closer we get to understanding this direct experience, the more humbling the process becomes, and the more we can begin to explore the issues of birth, life, and death. *Who am I? Where did I come from? What is this thing called life—this immensity that I seem to be walking around in and breathing air from and constantly dealing with? What is life? What is this thing I call the world, the universe, or the cosmos?* Questions of birth and life naturally lead us to questions of death. *What is death beyond my fear of it? What is the reality of it?* Not your death, but any death: *What is happening when death occurs?*

Death is a radical moment of change. Life is no longer taking that form, the form of whatever died, whether it is you, a loved one, an animal, an insect, a leaf that floats from a tree, or an apple that falls to the ground. The essence of death is a change, a transformation, and it is happening constantly. Life depends on this, for life is movement, it is change, it is like a burning flame, and it is not static. Birth, life, and death are ways of describing change or transmutation: one thing becoming another thing, the tree trunk becoming the forest floor again, being reabsorbed, breaking down into elements, only to become part of what fuels another tree or another blade of grass. In this sense, life itself is eternal. Yes, it is always changing, as it is impermanent by its very nature, but death is not what we imagine it to be.

Death is the end of life taking a specific form. When life no longer takes that form, we may miss that form, we may grieve for it, and it may cut to the bone to let go of a form that life took—the form of a loved one, child, grandmother, grandfather, best friend, lover, wife, or husband. I do not mean to diminish this, but the reality of that being—the reality of that life, the suchness of it—is endless and deathless. Life does not go from something to nothing; we know because science tells us that. Things change form, but there is never more or less life. If we identify strictly with a particular form, then death will seem like a catastrophe, and we will start grasping for ways to get out of death, to survive, and to somehow slip through the net of change. I may think I will inhabit various life-forms, the way a pilot can sit in the seats of different planes or a driver can slip in and out of different cars; there are many ways that human beings try to cheat the reality of death. However, the reality is not what we have been told; the reality is not about endings, but it is about transformations, about life transforming from one form into the next.

Life is a constant process of birth and death. Birth itself is life changing from one form into another. Life does not begin when you come out of your mother's womb, and it does not end when your heart stops beating; birth is happening continuously, life is happening continuously, and death is happening continuously. The enlightened perspective is to see that we are the whole, yet we are also life taking a particular form. This is not a denial of that particular form; people think that unity is somehow a denial of uniqueness or distinctiveness, but it is not. Life does take unique forms, as one form does not look like the other on the surface, in the realm of sight, smell, taste, and touch. One form is distinct from another form—a tree looks different from a rock, and a rock is different from a human being—but they are all composed of life. I am using the word "life" here to encompass everything that is.

It takes an entire universe to create a human being. If there is no universe, then there is no me, and there is no you. To return to my analogy of the wave, you are like one wave in an ocean, but you are also the ocean, because the wave is entirely formed of the ocean, and it never leaves the ocean. There is no such thing as a wave floating six feet above the surface of the ocean, cut off from it. The wave is always connected: it is the ocean, and it is the ocean waving. Our life is like a wave: it begins, and then the wave one day washes up against the shore, and that form disappears. Is there any less water? No. But is the wave itself gone? Yes, completely gone. If we liked that particular wave we may miss it, and we may grieve that the ocean is no longer taking that form.

This is different from our conventional view of death, which is that when someone dies they snap out of existence. If you have ever been with someone who is dying, you know that the changing of the form, the moment of death, is discernable. Even if in that moment when it happens you have your eyes closed, you know; it is a powerful moment. It is an honor to be present when someone passes, as it is a profoundly deep and moving experience, but death is experienced differently when we know that life does not disappear as the form disappears. This is why people can lose a loved one and suddenly feel their loved one everywhere. We think of that as a poetic experience—the human imagination projecting the memory of somebody we've loved—and as something we do with our mind and our ideas, but there is also a reality to it beyond the ideas. That person always was life, and although the form life took has disappeared, the life itself is everywhere. To feel that someone is everywhere is not merely a romantic comfort created by those who are grieving. It touches a fundamental reality: the forms change, and there is a definitive moment of the changing of the form, but there is no more and no less life.

When a Christian contemplates the reality of Christ, if they go deep, eventually they will begin to realize that Christ was not a historical figure. History tells us there was someone named Jesus and life took the form of that man, or perhaps God took that form, but Jesus—transcendent of the form—was all of life all along. In the noncanonical early Christian text the Gospel of Thomas, Jesus said, "Split wood, I am there. Lift up a rock, you will find me there." Many accounts tell of Christian contemplatives discovering the reality of Christ everywhere, including in the form of their own body. There are also accounts of Buddhists suddenly realizing that their body is the Buddha, and so is every other body and everything else. This realization is not exclusive, and it is not, "I am the Buddha, and you are not"—that is still a delusion.

"Buddha" is a word for that which gives rise to all forms, is all forms, and survives the changing of forms. It is the essence, the reality, and the suchness. I am trying to use a conventional, unflashy word by calling it "life." Life transcends all forms. I had that experience of chasing my Buddha nature (as we would say in Buddhism) everywhere, looking around, looking inside me, looking all over, until I suddenly realized, *I am the Buddha nature. All of me is the Buddha nature.* And all of *you* is the Buddha nature, and all of existence is the Buddha nature, and absence of existence is the Buddha nature. What a freeing and liberating discovery! There is no longer fear of death once we have seen that and live with it day to day, because death does not mean essential endings. There is no more or less of life, and there is no more or less of you.

It is said that when people were lamenting Ramana Maharshi's impending death from cancer, he asked, "Why are you so attached to this body? Where can I go? I am here." He already had identification with the universal; or, as he said, there is only the self. I am using the word "life" in the same way he used the word "self"—there is only the self. "Where can I go?" Everywhere is already the self or life. Just because the self stops taking the form that we call Ramana does not mean the self disappears out of existence. The self is still perfectly present everywhere and in everything. The form of Ramana changed, died, or passed away, but the self—the entirety of that form, right down to its biology and chemistry and what transcends its biology and chemistry—is everywhere. It does not exist more in India than in the middle of San Francisco, or Pittsburgh, or Amsterdam, or Paris, or on top of a green mountain, or in a beautiful Buddhist temple, or inside a church that has known centuries of worship. When we see the reality of things, we stop bickering about what is the true form and what is not.

Our true nature does not come into being at birth, and it does not go out of being at death; only our form, the form that life adopted, comes into being at birth and goes out of existence at death. This is why when we awaken, when we are realized, we know there is no birth or death in some essential sense; there is the changing of forms, but not the beginning and the end of one's existence. So in Zen, when they say the real reason for the whole spiritual endeavor is to resolve the Great Matter of birth, life, and death, they mean it.

I promise you there is a resolution to the Great Matter of birth, life, and death. This realization does not get you out of the challenges of life and living or of birth or dying. It does not mean you will never grieve the passing of someone, but it will be different when you do not mistakenly think that what they were is gone. The form they took is gone, and you may have loved the form and cherished the form—just as you may miss the self or the Buddha nature or life taking that form—but there is no more or less life, there is no more or less Buddha nature, and there is no more or less Christ. This is a wholly different way to experience birth, life, and death: it is not a denial of these things, but it is seeing what they are, and therefore it is liberating. Your form will go out of being—with or without realization—but the reality of you does not come into or go out of anything.

I say this by way of encouraging self-exploration. You can believe what I teach or you can disbelieve it—that is your prerogative—but neither one is significant. If you believe it, it is no more significant than disbelieving it, because to believe something is not the same as experiencing it, and to disbelieve something is not the same as experiencing it. As long as we are caught in the realm of acceptance and rejection, believing and disbelieving, we are living in a world of abstraction. That is what spiritual teachers mean—at least it is what I mean—by saying we are living in a dream. Therefore, believing or disbelieving is not the point.

I encourage you to have a profound and genuine curiosity, a deep determination to go beyond the world that is created by concepts and ideas (as useful as they can be), and an intention to wake up from living an abstract life—from liking what your mind tells you to like, disliking what your mind tells you to dislike, agreeing with what your conditioned mind tells you to agree with, disagreeing with what your conditioned mind tells you to disagree with, and everything endlessly looping in a waking dream. Much of the genuine spiritual impulse comes from dissatisfaction with living in that dream. The real instinct for enlightenment or awakening or God comes from a kind of dissatisfaction—from no longer wanting to live an abstracted life, no longer wanting your life to continue to contribute to the world of sorrow, and paying attention to the desire to have a rich and deep experience of being instead of one created by what you believe. This is the real enlightenment impulse.

I hope I have given you some helpful hints about how to go about this, about how to dive underneath the conditioned world and the imagined ego self to your true nature, because we are all Buddhas; there is only the Buddha, and there is only the self. Christ is everywhere you look. Jesus the man, the form Christ took, was born, lived, and died, but the Christ that Jesus was through and through to the marrow is everywhere all the time—we are all children of God in that respect. The clamoring and the desperate, angst-ridden search for the divine occurs when we are convinced that the divine lies somewhere outside of right here and right now. Make your search one of curiosity: reconnect with your sense of wonder and of awe, go into the still places inside of you, and let yourself be taken underneath the conceptual mind. Trust the quiet spaces within, because they are the ultimate sutras of existence.

About the Author

Adyashanti is an American-born spiritual teacher devoted to serving the awakening of all beings. His teachings are an open invitation to stop, inquire, and recognize what is true and liberating at the core of all existence. His books include *Emptiness Dancing*, *The End of Your World*, *True Meditation*, *The Way of Liberation*, *Falling into Grace*, and *Resurrecting Jesus*.

Asked to teach in 1996 by his Zen teacher of fourteen years, Adyashanti offers teachings that are free of any tradition or ideology. "The Truth I point to is not confined within any religious point of view, belief system, or doctrine, but is open to all and found within all."

For more information, please visit adyashanti.org.

About Sounds True

Sounds True is a multimedia publisher whose mission is to inspire and support personal transformation and spiritual awakening. Founded in 1985 and located in Boulder, Colorado, we work with many of the leading spiritual teachers, thinkers, healers, and visionary artists of our time. We strive with every title to preserve the essential "living wisdom" of the author or artist. It is our goal to create products that not only provide information to a reader or listener, but that also embody the quality of a wisdom transmission.

For those seeking genuine transformation, Sounds True is your trusted partner. At SoundsTrue.com you will find a wealth of free resources to support your journey, including exclusive weekly audio interviews, free downloads, interactive learning tools, and other special savings on all our titles.

To learn more, please visit SoundsTrue.com/freegifts or call us toll-free at 800.333.9185.

SOUNDS TRUE
many voices, one journey